The Organization of an

ALASKAN EXPEDITION

The Organization of an

ALASKAN EXPEDITION

Boyd N. Everett, Jr.

Gorak Books
Pasadena, California

4

Published by Gorak Books
                    P.O. Box 5411
                    Pasadena, California 91107

Printed in the United States of America

Library of Congress Cataloging in Publication Data

Everett, Boyd N., 1933-1969.
    The organization of an Alaskan expedition.

    Bibliography: p.
    Includes index.
        1. Mountaineering--Alaska--Organization and
            management.
    2. Mountaineering--Yukon Territory--Organization and
        management.
    I. Title
    GV199.42.A4E88   1984   796.5'22'09798   84-80852
    ISBN 0-918803-00-4

Maps by Frances White, SHCJ
Typesetting by: The Typeshop
Cover: The Summit Ridge of Mt. Logan
        Photo by Barbara Lilley.
Frontispiece: On the East Buttress of Mt. McKinley.
        Photo by Bill Krause.

TABLE OF CONTENTS

6

PUBLISHER'S NOTE

Boyd N. Everett, Jr., presented this paper on March 4, 1966 at a seminar of the Harvard Mountaineering Club. Since that time it has been regarded as the best source of information on the preparation of a mountaineering expedition to Alaska and the Yukon. While this report has been described as "timeless," this version has been edited and updated to be more timely with expedition practices in the 1980's. Sections on regulations, equipment, and mountains and routes have been completely updated, with a few exceptions. We couldn't resist including Everett's opinions on ten point versus twelve point crampons, ice axes, food and other comments that may make this report seem somewhat dated. We included these items to remind the reader that this report was written in 1966 and this should help put in perspective current expedition practices in Alaska and the Yukon. Climbers who have learned alpinism on smaller peaks should have no difficulty differentiating between those sentences applicable to the 1960's and the 1980's.

A new section has been added: mountain ethics. In 1966 there were less than a hundred climbers in the Alaska Range and St. Elias Mountains. Now there are almost a thousand every year. Climbers can no longer assume that no one will be effected by their expedition waste. Anyone reading this report and climbing in Alaska or the Yukon will be expected to leave the mountains clean.

After considerable discussion and spirited debate, we decided to use the European names for mountains, rather than native Alaskan names. The State of Alaska Board of Geographic Names and most Alaskans (native and otherwise) now refer to Mt. McKinley as "Denali," the Athabascan name meaning "The High One." The United States Board of Domestic Geographic Names still refers to the mountain at 63°04' North, 151°00' West as "Mt. McKinley." Our decision to use European names is based on the hope that this will create less confusion. We apologize to those we have offended by this decision.

Everett probably had some assistance when he originally prepared this work and we wish that we could acknowledge these people here. This updated version has been critically reviewed by Robert Somoano and Bill Krause. Robert Gerhard of Denali National Park and Preserve, Charles Budge of Wrangell — St. Elias National Park and Preserve, Donald Chase of Glacier Bay National Park and Preserve, and Lloyd Freese of Kluane National Park reviewed the "Regulations" and "Mountain Ethics" sections and offered many suggestions that will help expeditions minimize their impact in the mountains.

This report is not a treatise on mountaineering technique. It will be of assistance to experienced climbers in preparation of a mountaineering expedition once they have learned their craft on smaller mountains under competent instruction. This report is no substitute for mountaineering skill, experience or judgement. Inexperienced mountaineers are encouraged to spend several seasons on lesser peaks before attempting ascents of the greatest mountains in the North American cordillera: the Alaska Range and the St. Elias Mountains.

Gorak Books

The Organization of an

ALASKAN EXPEDITION

Mt. St. Elias from the Newton Glacier (Barbara Lilley photo)

SCOPE AND PURPOSE OF THIS REPORT

It is hoped that this report can be of practical help to groups or individuals planning expeditions to Alaska or the St. Elias Mountains of the Yukon. Climbing conditions in these areas are essentially identical and general comments apply to both areas. When one refers to Alaskan mountaineering the reference is to a style of mountaineering and not to climbing in a specific political division. Therefore, by definition and for simplicity, the words "Alaska" or "Alaskan" in this report will automatically encompass the Yukon as well.

The press of a specific time deadline made it necessary to research and write this report in two weeks. Therefore the writer makes no representation that it is a complete or an authoritative discussion of the topic. There are undoubtedly some inaccuracies in it, particularly in the final section on routes and the grading of climbs. Corrections and suggestions will be gratefully accepted.

Rarely do pure technical difficulties exceed the technical competence of an Alaskan expedition. For those expeditions that are not successful the two most common scapegoats are bad weather and avalanche dangers. Almost without exception, however, the real causes of expedition failure are bad group morale or bad organization. When either morale or organization break down, it is certainly convenient to use a stretch of bad weather or a temporary objective hazard as an excuse to call the project off. The contingency of bad weather can be allowed for and permanent hazards, such as hanging glaciers, should be visible in advance and thus avoidable. This report can do little about group morale, except to emphasize its importance, but hopefully it can be of some practical aid in planning so that some of the most common errors can be avoided. It is the writer's opinion that the more difficult new routes will require more attention to organizational details than most expeditions have made in the past.

The Abruzzi Ridge on Mt. St. Elias (Barbara Lilley photo)

THE PARTY AND ITS LEADERSHIP

This is not the place to argue about the merits of large or small parties. In practice the most common size for an expedition is six. This allows two ropes of three for glacier travel and three ropes of two on technical ice or rock. Expeditions of less than four cannot be encouraged here. Kluane National Park requires that a group must have at least four members, and at one time Denali National Park & Preserve required a minimum of four members. This is one regulation that makes sense because the remoteness of Alaskan mountains requires that a party be able to evacuate any injured party member by itself.

Probably the most important factor in choosing a party for an expedition is that every individual be congenial and able to live with every other individual under strenuous conditions for a period of weeks. Social compatibility is essential. It will almost never pay to take the exceptionally strong but humorless and unresponsive technician over a congenial but less technically oriented climber. For most routes it is probably best to have a party of similar technical ability and physical strength. Particularly when the party is young, similar age groups may be desirable. On potentially difficult routes it may seem desirable to have a few climbers of exceptional ability for the difficult leading. This can work out but the risk of an unequal party must be recognized. In practice the stronger climbers may become impatient with the slowness of the lesser climbers. The weaker climbers may begin to feel pressed by the stronger climbers and in some cases may resent their ability to do more. Where there are disparities in ability the better climbers usually do the best leading and this can cause resentment.

Several non-American climbers run expeditions with military discipline. The writer has no opinion whether this military discipline works for the nationalities that use it. The few American expeditions that have been run on military lines, however, have usually not been too successful. Americans in general and American climbers in particular just don't respond well to rigid discipline. We are too independent minded. Most American climbers would probably prefer to have no expedition leader and to make all decisions by majority vote. This can work if all of the expedition members are nearly equal in ability and experience (and probably age as well) and if the whole group has had some previous experience working in this way with each other. Unless the group knows that group consent can be obtained harmoniously under what may be adverse conditions, however, there is considerable risk in this arrangement. For example, what happens when a party of six splits three and three on an issue involving the safety of the expedition?

Most expeditions will probably have a nominal leader. In Denali National Park & Preserve and Kluane National Park it is legally required. It is strongly recommended that whatever authority and responsibility the leader will have should be thoroughly talked out and settled before the expedition starts, not in a storm blown tent high on the mountain. The writer has had one bad experience because the limits of the leader's authority were not clearly understood until a difference of opinion arose on the mountain.

The writer's philosophy about leadership can be expressed as follows: All men are created equal but some men are created more equal. This means that under most circumstances the leader's voice carries as much weight as any other expedition member. It would be the leader's job to coordinate operations — i.e., the leader is responsible for the expedition's efficiency — but he or she should do this by making suggestions, not by giving orders. The one occasion when the leader should give orders is when the safety of the party is in dispute and it is the leader's opinion that safety requires a certain action.

To repeat: Regardless of what authority the leader is to have, this should be discussed in advance. The size of the party and the remoteness of the mountain make it unwise to have the casual understandings about leadership that are common among ropes of two or three in the continental United States.

PLANNING THE ROUTE

In choosing an Alaskan route it is likely that most climbers will be unnecessarily conservative in estimating what they can do technically. The size of most Alaskan mountains seems to make even good technical climbers more cautious. Caution is in practice warranted when evaluating possible avalanche hazards but pure technical problems often work out more easily than anticipated. Alaskan climbs are expensive and many climbers get only one chance to climb there in their lifetimes. A warm-up climb is often not possible. Therefore the writer recommends that climbers of reasonable technical competency and mountain experience be fairly aggressive in choosing routes — recognizing, however, that they may be "psyched out" at first by the size of the mountain and that objective hazards must be carefully evaluated. The more aggressive the route the more important organization becomes.

Some climbers worry about their ability to do climbing at higher elevations. For the great majority of climbers acclimitization up to altitudes of 20,000' (6100 m) is fairly easy. As some of the best routes in South America have shown, altitude is not a bar to good technical climbing.

To help choose a route there is a great deal of information available. It is possible to find pictures of every significant Alaskan mountain. Good photographs suitable for route planning are available for a majority of routes on the significant mountains. For mountains and routes that have been climbed the best source is usually the *American Alpine Journal.* There is a picture of almost every major climbed mountain in the *AAJ,* usually in the year following the first ascent. A list of mountains, routes, and the year of their first ascent appears in the final section of this report. In addition to the *AAJ,* the *Canadian Alpine Journal,* various other climbing club journals and *The Mountain World* may have useful photographs.

The best source of Alaskan photographs for study is the world famous collection of Bradford Washburn. This collection consists of over five thousand negatives and includes all of the major mountains and glaciers in the Alaska Range, Chugach Mountains, Wrangell Mountains, St. Elias Mountains, and the Fairweather Range. Black and white prints can be ordered from:

Boston's Museum of Science
Attention: Bradford Washburn
Science Park
Boston, Massachusetts   02114-1099 USA

Adequate, but not 100% accurate topographic maps in scales of 1:250,000, 1:63,360, or 1:50,000 are available from the United States and Canadian governments. The United States mailing address is:

Western Distribution Branch
U.S. Geological Survey
Box 25286, Denver Federal Center
Denver, Colorado   80225 USA

The Canadian mailing address is:
Canada Map Office
Surveys and Mapping Branch
Department of Energy, Mines and Resources
615 Booth Street
Ottawa, Ontario   K1A 0E9 CANADA

Area	1:250,000 Scale Maps
Alaska Range, Mt. Spurr	U.S., Tyonek, Alaska
" , Revelation Mtns.	" Lime Hills, Alaska
" , Kichatna Mtns.	" Talkeetna, Alaska
" , Mt. McKinley	" Mt. McKinley, Alaska
" , Mt. Deborah	" Healy, Alaska
" , Mt. Kimball	" Mt. Hayes, Alaska
Chugach Mtns.,	U.S.,
Mt. Marcus Baker	Anchorage, Alaska
" , Mt. Witherspoon	" Valdez, Alaska
" , Mt. Steller	" Bering Glacier, Alaska

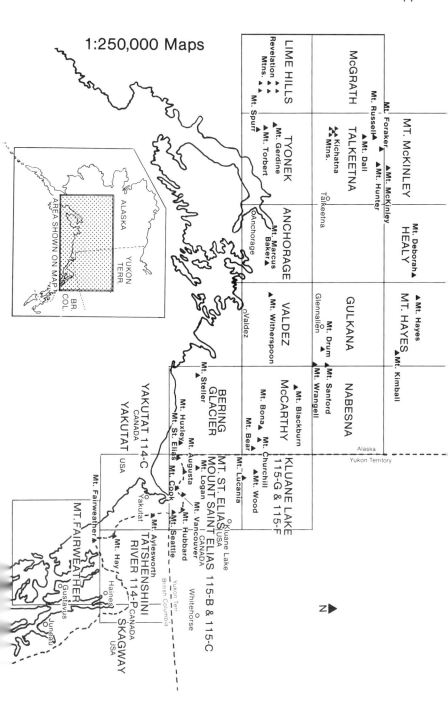

1:250,000 Maps

Area	**1:250,000 Scale Maps**

Wrangell Mtns., Mt.Wrangell U.S., Gulkana, Alaska
    "   , Mt. Sanford   "   Nabesna, Alaska
    "   , Mt. Blackburn   "   McCarthy, Alaska

St. Elias Mtns., Mt. Bona   U.S., McCarthy, Alaska
    "   , Mt. Huxley   "   Bering Glacier, Alaska
    "   , Mt. Vancouver   "   Mt. St. Elias, Alaska
    "   , Mt. Aylesworth   "   Yakutat, Alaska
    "   , Mt. Hay   "   Skagway, Alaska
    "   , Mt. Fairweather   "   Mt. Fairweather, Alaska
    "   , Mt. Wood   Canada: Kluane Lake, 115G
                                       & 115F
    "   , Mt. Logan   "   Mount St. Elias,
                                115B & 115C
    "   , Mt. Aylesworth   "   Yakutat 114-O
    "   , Mt. Lodge   "   Tatshenshini River
                                    114 P

For general use the Sectional Aeronautical Charts (1:500,000) and World Aeronautical Charts (1:1,000,000) can be helpful. Sectional Aeronautical Charts "McGrath," "Anchorage," "Whitehorse," "Juneau," and World Aeronautical Charts "CD-11," and "CD-12" cover all of the climbing areas. They can be obtained from:

Distribution Division, OA/C44
National Ocean Survey, NOAA
Riverdale, Maryland   20737 USA

Whereas climbers often overestimate the pure technical difficulty of a route there is a definite tendency to underestimate how many days a route will take to climb. Climbers accustomed to looking at 2,000' and 3,000' (600 m and 900 m) vertical rises in the Canadian Rockies will have difficulty gauging distances when they look at photos of Alaska's 8,000' to 10,000' (2400 m to 3000 m) (and larger) vertical rises. Even when the mountains are properly evaluated for size, climbers usually overestimate their ability to move in them. There are several reasons for this. For many climbers there are psychological barriers to efficient work initially. Uncertainty about climbing and avalanche conditions is a factor. Low altitude climbing done at night will be slower than similar climbing in daylight. On the bigger mountains, altitudes will slow the party somewhat, particularly while backpacking. There is a tendency to underestimate the time required for camp chores. Meals usually require two or more hours. Breaking each camp, including a meal, takes three to four hours. It shouldn't take this long but it does. Six hours for eating and camp chores per day plus eight hours for sleeping leaves only ten hours per day, sometimes less, for actual climbing. This compares with twelve to fourteen hours for most other mountains. Weather factors will often shorten or limit the efficiency of many climbing days.

A not bad rule of thumb in estimating the length of an expedition is to calculate the number of *climbing* days the route ought to require under good conditions and multiply by two. With any luck on weather a strong and efficient party usually will do the climb in less than twice the optimum number of climbing days but this gives a safety factor. If the party has no urgent time problem and wants to be certain of the summit, they might add five days (and food for five days) to the total. It would be unusual for bad weather to make over half of all the days unclimbable. The average party, even if less than half the days are bad, will need extra time to allow for mistakes in route finding, personal illness and imperfect use of available time. Normal climber errors must be allowed for.

For routes that have already been done, climbing time can be judged by the experience of previous parties, allowing for their ability and climbing philosophies. In general a second ascent ought to require a few days less than the first ascent assuming all other factors to be equal.

The best way to calculate climbing days on a new route is to first pick out campsites. If a site seems satisfactory in a picture, it can usually be counted on while on the mountain, provided there is no avalanche danger. In practice many campsites exist on the mountain that are not obvious in photos. Nevertheless it is better in choosing routes to make sure that suitable campsites are a realistic distance from each other. There is a tendency to plan on putting campsites too far apart. The mountain will often dictate the spacing of campsites but the following is a

Approaching King Col on Mt. Logan (Barbara Lilley photo)

rough guide of *maximum* desirable vertical distances between campsites. These distances assume moderately easy technical problems and no long traverses in deep snow, a common problem between 12,000' and 15,000' (3700 m and 4600 m).

Below 12,000' (3700 m)	3,000' (900 m) gain
12,000' — 15,000' (3700 m — 4600 m)	2,500' (800 m) gain
Above 15,000' (4600 m)	2,000' (600 m) gain

On the summit day a vertical rise in excess of 3,000' (900 m), even without a heavy load, is considered marginal.

The above distances assume only a single carry between campsites. Some trail breakers will have difficulty getting even this far in one day if snow conditions are bad. Load carrying over a packed trail goes faster than trail breaking unloaded but not nearly as fast as normal climbing in the western United States without a pack. This obvious fact is overlooked by many in judging how far apart campsites should be placed. As a rule of thumb, assuming average technical problems, snow conditions and weather, the vertical distances noted above will require four to six hours with a fifty pound (23 kg) load (with perhaps two 10 minute rest stops). The trail breaker, if carrying a load as well, may need at least 50% more time. Descending unloaded will require only 25% to 35% of the ascent time unless technical problems require much belaying. On horizontal traverses, 1½ mph (2.4 kph) is pretty good time unless the surface is very hard. Ten miles (16 km) of level glacier travel is a fair day's work. The old rule of thumb of two horizontal miles (3.2 km) and a thousand vertical feet (300 m) per hour doesn't work.

After picking probable campsites some estimate of the number of loads between campsites must be made. This can best be done by estimating the total weight of the expedition and allowing for reduced food and equipment as the expedition moves up the mountain. Two common errors are to overestimate the weight that *each* climber can carry *every* day. It is a very rare party that can carry 75 lbs. (34 kg) comfortably day after day. Fifty pounds (23 kg) every day is much more comfortable and can be carried without the occasional need for an enforced rest day. Only storm days should be rest days. As for total weight, climbers tend to forget several important facts. The amount of food carried is not the minimum, namely twenty days of food for a ten day climb. Food weight can be increased at least 25% by packaging. Personal gear may weigh 35 to 50 lbs. (15 to 23 kg), at least at base camp, and probably represents a nearly full load. The weight of the pack must be added to each load. All hardware is heavy, although it packs well. Fixed rope, fuel, the medical kit and spare equipment all add up. To repeat — realism is needed in setting distances between campsites and in estimating how many loads need to be carried.

The Northwest Ridge of Mt. Huntington (Bill Krause photo)

REGULATIONS

Most of the major Alaska mountains are under government regulation. While most climbers would prefer that climbing not be regulated, the administration of climbing has so far been reasonable, in the writer's opinion. It will probably remain so unless individual climbers cause difficulty by breaking the rules that do exist.

Denali National Park and Preserve

This area includes Mt. McKinley, Mt. Foraker, Mt. Hunter, Mt. Huntington, The Moose's Tooth, Mt. Dan Beard, Mt. Russell, and the Kichatna Mountains. The following regulations must be complied with by expeditions planning climbs of Mt. McKinley and Mt. Foraker, and are recommended for other climbs within the park.

The leader of the expedition must register with the Mountaineering Ranger at or before the start of the climb. Each climber must submit an individual registration briefly listing previous climbing experience and major ascents. These registration forms may be submitted to the Mountaineering Rangers in advance of the climb in order that the staff can evaluate the group's capability and offer advice and assistance. Or these forms can simply be prepared at the Talkeetna Ranger Station or Denali Park Headquarters at the start of the climb. To simplify correspondence, each party must have a distinct name and all communications with the National Park Service, glacier pilots, or support organizations must refer to that name.

Each expedition should report to Denali Park Head-quarters or to the Talkeetna Ranger Station by phone or in person just prior to departure and immediately after return from the climb.

All climbing parties must remove all litter and equip-ment waste from the park. All fuel and food containers and damaged equipment (including fixed ropes) must be packed out. Caches of food, fuel or equipment must be removed from the park's backcountry.

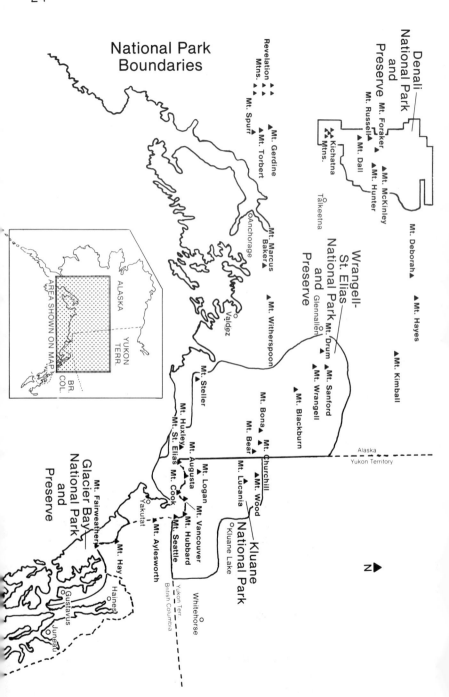

National Park
Boundaries

Denali National Park and Preserve

Wrangell-St. Elias National Park and Preserve

Glacier Bay National Park and Preserve

Kluane National Park

Revelation Mtns.

Kichatna Mtns.

▲Mt. Foraker
▲Mt. Russell
▲Mt. Spurr
▲Mt. Gerdine
▲Mt. Torbert
▲Mt. Dall
▲Mt. McKinley
▲Mt. Hunter
Mt. Deborah▲
▲Mt. Hayes
▲Mt. Kimball

○Talkeetna
○Anchorage
○Valdez
○Glennallen

▲Mt. Marcus Baker
▲Mt. Witherspoon
Mt. Drum▲
▲Mt. Sanford
▲Mt. Wrangell
▲Mt. Blackburn
Mt. Steller▲
Mt. Bona▲
Mt. Bear▲
▲Mt. Churchill
▲Mt. Wood

Mt. Huxley▲
Mt. St. Elias▲
Mt. Augusta▲
Mt. Logan▲
Mt. Lucania

Mt. Cook▲
Mt. Vancouver▲
Mt. Hubbard▲
Mt. Seattle▲

Mt. Fairweather▲
○Yakutat
▲Mt. Aylesworth
Mt. Hay▲

○Kluane Lake
○Whitehorse

Alaska
Yukon Territory

Yukon Terr.
British Columbia

○Gustavus
○Haines
○Juneau

N▶

ALASKA
YUKON TERR.
BR. COL.
AREA SHOWN ON MAP

There are strict restrictions on aircraft landings and air drops in Denali National Park. Further information can be obtained by writing:

Mountaineering Ranger
Denali National Park and Preserve
P.O. Box 9
Denali Park, Alaska   99755   USA

Wrangell — St. Elias National Park and Preserve

This park includes the Wrangell Mountains, the eastern portion of the Chugach Mountains, and the St. Elias Mountains within Alaska. Climbing parties should register with park authorities. Airplanes are allowed to land anywhere within the park and preserve in support of mountaineering expeditions. Helicopter landings require a special permit. All litter, including wands, fixed ropes, food and equipment caches must be removed from the park and preserve. For more information, contact:

Wrangell — St. Elias National Park and Preserve
P.O. Box 29
Glennallen, Alaska   99588   USA

Glacier Bay National Park and Preserve

This park includes the Fairweather Range of the St. Elias Mountains in southeast Alaska. No airdrops are allowed and aircraft are only allowed to land on salt water, except at Adams Inlet. North of Sea Otter Creek (just north of Cape Fairweather) aircraft may land on fresh water or on the beach below the high tide mark. All garbage and damaged equipment must be removed from the back-country. Climbing parties should register with park authorities. For more information, contact:

Glacier Bay National Park and Preserve
Gustavus, Alaska   99828 USA

Kluane National Park

This area includes the St. Elias Mountains within the Yukon Territory of Canada. The following regulations must be complied with by mountaineering expeditions within Kluane National Park.

The leader of the expedition must apply to the Park Superintendent for a permit at least three months in advance of their planned arrival in the park. The application must include: 1) name of the expedition, expedition plan and route; 2) a complete list of equipment, personnel and man-days of food; 3) confirmation of air support; 4) confirmation of radio communication. Each individual expedition member must complete an application which includes: name, age, responsibilities in the expedition, address and telephone, emergency notification, club affiliation, blood type and a brief climbing resume. Each member must also submit a physician's certificate, stating that the climber is physically fit and able to participate in the expedition.

A group must have at least four members. (In 1950 Logan was climbed by a party of two but this would probably not be allowed today.) Seventy-five percent of the group must be experienced mountaineers. The leader must have extensive mountaineering and leadership experience. The leader must know the physical qualifications, condition and experience of each team member and be prepared to verify claims made by the members on their application forms.

All parties are required to carry radios, and the expedition must notify the Park Superintendent upon return.

All litter, including wands, fixed ropes, food and equipment caches must be removed from Kluane National Park.

All of these regulations are strictly enforced. Application forms and correspondence should be directed to:

Superintendent
Kluane National Park
Parks Canada
Haines Junction, Yukon Territory Y0B 1L0
CANADA

TRANSPORTATION

Daily jet service is available to Anchorage from most major cities of North America, Europe, and east Asia. Commercial passenger flights are available to Whitehorse via Edmonton, Vancouver, Fairbanks or Juneau. During the summer, there is bus service up the Alcan Highway (also known as the Alaska Highway) from Edmonton.

Some expeditions like to have at least one car, preferably a van or station wagon, to transport food and expedition gear. Driving to Dawson Creek, British Columbia is on good, paved highways. The Alcan Highway from Dawson Creek is an improved dirt road, some sections of which are in good condition and can be driven comfortably at fifty miles per hour (80 kph). Other sections may be poor and require driving at thirty miles per hour (50 kph). Forty miles per hour (65 kph) is a good average speed over the entire road. From Dawson Creek it is approximately 1,050 miles (1690 km) to Kluane Lake, 1,418 miles (2283 km) to Glennallen, and 1,602 miles (2579 km) to Anchorage.

The Alcan is quite hard on most cars, particularly older ones. Some repairs must be expected. Gasoline is expensive on some remote parts of the Alcan, and minor repairs and a new tire or two should be planned for when preparing the expedition budget. Major repairs can take several days on the Alcan since parts must often be brought from Edmonton.

Some climbers have tried buying a car in the continental United States and selling it in Alaska. Very few have done well financially because they have not had the time to shop for a good price and because competition from other car sellers is keen during the summer.

Passing through Canadian customs is no problem but there are a few caveats. Technically no one is supposed to carry more than a few days of food in the car. There is a danger of paying a heavy duty for expedition food. Most customs officers probably would not bother climbers but those at remote crossings don't have much to enliven their day except to harass tourists. Custom crossings are usually easier at major ports of entry. Customs will ask about liquor and cigarettes as well.

While all of the supplies in the medical kit are probably

On the East Buttress of Mt. McKinley (Bill Krause photo)

legal, it is perhaps better not to have the kit conspicuously in the open, or in the glove compartment, where it is asking for questions.

All persons driving into Canada will have to prove that they have adequate resources to leave the country. This can include return air or bus tickets, credit cards, traveler's checks or cash. Entrance into Alaska will require proof of the same.

Talkeetna, Alaska, is the base of operations for Denali National Park and Preserve. It can be reached by auto or daily train from Anchorage. Some parties prefer to hire a limousine for direct transport from the Anchorage airport to Talkeetna. Denali National Park headquarters is located on the north side of the park at Denali Park and can be reached by road or train.

Glennallen, Alaska, is the base for the eastern Alaska Range, the Wrangell Mountains and a major part of the St. Elias and Chugach Mountains. It is on the Glenn Highway between Anchorage and Delta Junction. It can be reached in the summer by air or bus.

Yakutat, Alaska, is the closest town to much of the St. Elias Mountains. It can only be reached by air. Yakutat has incredibly bad weather and is not ideal as a base of operation.

Kluane Lake, Yukon Territory, is convenient for the eastern half of the St. Elias Mountains provided that a pilot can be found to operate from there. Kluane Lake is on the Alcan Highway. It can be reached by bus or air. Most charter aircraft operate out of Whitehorse.

Haines, Alaska, can be used in the southern St. Elias Mountains and the Fairweather Range. There is occasional air and ferry transportation to Haines. Gustavus and Juneau have been used as bases for expeditions to the Fairweather Range. There is daily air transportation to Juneau and Gustavus in the summer, and twice weekly ferry transportation to Juneau.

Almost all parties fly into their mountains from one of the above bases of operation. Except on the north side of Mt. McKinley and Mt. Foraker, where it is required, few parties walk. There is almost no mountain region in Alaska that can't and hasn't been reached on foot but this is an arduous, time consuming job. Walk in distances range from twenty-five miles (40 km) on Mt. McKinley (northside) to over one hundred miles (160 km) in some parts of the St. Elias Mountains. When extra food and air drop support is included, walking in willl usually not save a great deal of money. Glacier walking is hot, rainy and tedious. It may toughen the physical condition of a party but a long walk can also tire it out. The low elevation of most Alaskan glaciers will be of little help in acclimitization. The writer agrees with the philosophy that walking in is for the masochist or truly impoverished.

*View of Mt. Logan on the sixth day of the walk-in
(Barbara Lilley photo)*

GLACIER FLYING

Every major Alaskan mountain has a good landing site for a ski-wheeled plane, although good sites do not exist at the base of every potential route. Photographs usually reveal safe landing areas. It must be remembered that areas below 5,000' (1500 m) will have wet, sticky snow after June 1 and will be bad up to 8,000' (2400 m) by July 1. Such areas need long downhill slopes with no crevasses for take-offs.

Denali National Park and all other national parks in Alaska and the Yukon have restrictions on aircraft landings and air drops within park boundaries. The boundaries of the Denali Wilderness of Denali National Park are such that this flying restriction is not much of a problem on the south and east sides of Mt. McKinley, but it is a real restriction on the north and west. Denali National Park at one time permitted air drops within the Denali Wilderness. This was very important to parties walking in from the north and greatly aided those doing the popular West Buttress of McKinley. Careful study is necessary to determine whether a proposed landing or air drop site will be allowed under the current park regulations.

Glaciers pilots are very busy in June and July, the popular months for McKinley. On occasion, bad weather will overload them with work. Therefore, parties should not plan on tight time schedules. As Don Sheldon once said, "This is waitin' country." Pilots operating out of Talkeetna generally charge on the basis of one way per person (including gear) for flying anywhere in the McKinley area. Air drops are charged at the same per flight rate. These rates are a pretty steep rate per hour (compared to other glacier pilots) but most climbers do not complain. It is difficult and sometimes dangerous work.

Glacier pilots operating out of Glennallen, Kluane Lake, or Whitehorse generally charge on a per hour basis. This is generally cheaper on a mileage basis than the per flight rate charged by the Talkeetna pilots.

Typical aircraft include the Cessna 180 and the supercharged Piper Cub. The Cessna flies at about 110-120 mph (177-193 kph) fully loaded compared to 90 mph (145 kph) for the Super Cub. The Super Cub carries one

On Mt. Logan (Barbara Lilley photo)

On Mt. Wrangell (Barbara Lilley photo)

passenger and gear. The Cessna can carry three passengers and a small load or two passengers plus full expedition gear for two. In general, the Cessna is more economical. If the landing area is tight or new for the pilot, he or she may require that the Super Cub be used on the first landing. When estimating flying costs, don't forget to add five or ten minutes for taking off and landing. The first landing in particular requires careful scouting.

Helicopters have been used in recent years in place of fixed-wing aircraft. Helicopters have a limited range and their typical rate could be two or three times that of a flight by an airplane. Careful study is needed to determine whether the benefits of a helicopter are outweighed by the sometimes enormous cost.

Some expeditions like to have a check flight half way through the expedition. Glacier pilots will do this at their usual flying rates. When estimating the cost of this flight add about twenty minutes for the pilot to find the party on the mountain. Simple signals between party and pilot should be arranged in advance.

A common mistake for an expedition is to underestimate the time it needs to be on the mountain so that it is still climbing when the pilot comes in at the appointed pick-up time. This is no disaster. A good pilot will look for the party on the mountain and should not immediately report it lost. However, it will cost an amount equal to the check flight. One other flying cost warning: if the weather is marginal on the days set aside for check flights or pick-up, the pilot may start for the mountain only to have to turn back. He or she may charge for this flying even though not productive for the expedition.

King Peak (Barbara Lilley photo)

CLIMBING CONDITIONS

Several factors are important in deciding on dates for an Alaskan expedition. It is probable that every mountain could be climbed in any month of the year but some months are decidedly inhospitable for obvious reasons. The following factors should be considered in choosing expedition dates.

Hours of Daylight

Between June 1 and July 15 there are nearly 24 hours of daylight in Alaska and the Yukon. The sun actually goes down for four hours but the twilight is usually bright enough for all night climbing. This has two important advantages. It permits evening climbing when daytime climbing would be hazardous because of sun induced avalanche conditions. It also permits the climber to begin and end the day whenever he or she wants and weather conditions permit. For example, if a storm ends at 2:00 pm, the climber can start to climb then whereas further south this day would be lost for climbing.

Before May 15 and after August 1 there are at least three hours of nearly total darkness. Outside of this date range, storms will upset climbing schedules because the opportunity to climb through the night will not exist.

Landing Site

Some landing sites are usuable througout the summer but crevasses or deep snow can make others impossible. The limiting factor is not the date the party goes in but the day it comes off the mountain. Nearly level glaciers, such as the Seward, are very sticky after July 1.

Weather Trends

The prevailing winds are out of the south and southwest off the ocean. It is understood that there are occasionally cold violent windstorms from the north but the writer has never seen one. The prevailing wind from the ocean usually carries warm air. When this warm air hits the mountains surrounded by glaciers, precipitation follows.

The warmer the temperature, the higher the probability of bad weather.

In the McKinley area there are likely to be a fair number of clear, but often cold and windy days in April and early May. Although it is 150 miles (240 km) from the ocean, McKinley is unprotected from the sea to the south.

Thus, by the end of May warm air from the ocean makes its way to McKinley and local storms develop. The weather, particularly on the southern side where the clouds often boil up, gets progressively worse until in late July and early August a completely clear day is a rarity. By September the weather is reportedly much better.

In the St. Elias and Chugach Mountains, the proximity of the mountains to the ocean makes warm ocean air a weather factor over a longer period. May, June and July all have a percentage of bad weather, perhaps 50% on average. The writer had excellent weather in early April, 1965, but this perhaps may have been luck. A winter storm is still possible this early in the year. It has been reported that August in the St. Elias Mountains has some excellent days but the writer cannot verify this.

The frequency of storms and amount of snowfall in these coastal mountains is in direct relation to the distance from the ocean. Thus Mt. St. Elias has worse weather than Mt. Logan and Mt. Logan has worse weather than Mt. Lucania. Each mountain shields the next mountain inland from some precipitation. There is a noticeable difference of weather on the north and south sides of the highest peaks.

In the Wrangell Mountains, which are protected from the ocean by the Chugach Mountains, there is a weather pattern similar to the interior ranges of British Columbia. Local clouds tend to be heavy from May to August (caused, the writer believes, by the heat in the Cooper River Valley). The weather in this region seems to be less violent but is also less stable. Storms of several days duration do not seem to be a normal recurrence.

Temperature Ranges

It is possible for all of the big mountains to have very cold temperatures, even in mid-summer. Temperatures of

Mt. St. Elias (Barbara Lilley photo)

-30°F (-34°C) have been recorded by climbers in June and July on McKinley and Logan. It does appear, however, that a minimum temperature of -10°F to -15°F (-23°C to -26°C) would be normal. The writer, in six years, has never recorded a temperature worse than -5°F (-20°C); this experience includes an early April ascent of Mt. King George (12,250';3734 m) and a June — July ascent of Mt. McKinley (20,320';6193 m). The disadvantage with April and September for climbing in spite of more clear days is that temperatures are colder. A temperature of -40°F (-40°C) has been recorded on McKinley in April. During the true winter months temperatures of -60°F to -70°F (-51°C to -56°C) can be recorded.

As a rule of thumb, one can assume the temperature will be 3°F colder for each thousand feet of elevation, or 1°C colder for each hundred meters of elevation. Air temperatures during the day at 8,000' (2400 m) in June and July average around 30°F (-1°C). The air temperature will drop 5°F to 10°F (2.75°C to 5.5°C) during the evening although the change will seem much greater if the sun has been shining. Temperatures inside the tents at midday can reach 70°F (21°C) because of the sun.

Because of the heat of the sun, snow slopes below 12,000' (3600 m) may be dangerous to climb during the day. It will be unpleasant, at least, to break trails or carry loads in the heat. Low altitude rock climbing, however, can be pleasant. Unfortunately most low altitude Alaskan rock is quite rotten.

There is a popular belief that the weather is Alaska changes very rapidly. There are elements of truth in this statement but it needs clarification. From a relatively clear sky a violent storm can appear within two hours. In such cases, however, there are almost always telltale signs for several hours previously. Such signs would include long cloud streaks in the sky and lenticular cloud caps over the high summits. When the weather is really clear it rarely turns bad in less than twelve hours. A completely good weather day has noticeable brightness in the air which a day of changing weather usually doesn't have.

Good and bad weather tends to come in cycles. Good weather can last three to six days while bad weather conditions of ten consecutive days are not usual. During this bad weather period there will be some temporary clearings. Heavy clouds at lower or higher elevations or on other mountains will indicate that the bad weather may return. When it does return the change in condition can be sudden.

At low elevation, usually not above 8,000' (2400 m), climbers may also be annoyed by clouds that hang no more than 1,000' (300 m) above the glacier. These clouds which "creep" in off the ocean, bring whiteout and light rain or snow. They often appear when the weather higher on the mountains is excellent. These clouds, which are most common in July, can interfere with glacier flying and landings.

It should be no surprise that wind will interfere with climbing more often than falling snow. If routes are marked with wands or if whiteout conditions aren't too bad, climbing can be done at low elevations even during snow storms. When the wind does blow, however, it can be very violent, possibly up to 100 mph (160 kph) at higher elevations. The prevailing wind will be from the south or southwest but currents around the mountain can create strong gusts from any direction.

Snow fall will be heavy during storms. One to two feet (30-60 cm) of snow in a 24 hour period or three feet (90 cm) in two days is not unusual. It is normal to have at least a short break for a few hours after three days of continuous snow but the storm can easily return after the break. Ten feet (3 m) of powder snow in ten days is possible although this would consolidate into perhaps five feet (1.5 m) of solid snow. In general, there is no such thing as a partly cloudy day. There is either a clear sky or it snows.

Avalanche on Mt. Logan (Barbara Lilley photo)

Icefall beneath Russell Col (Barbara Lilley photo)

OBJECTIVE HAZARDS

Avalanches are the most important hazard that Alaskan climbers must be concerned with. Below about 12,000' (3600 m) the sun is an important factor even though the temperature remains well below freezing. South facing slopes, where the sun hits directly onto the snow, can become saturated with water. A slide similar to a mud slide can develop. Generally these saturation slides are not large nor do they extend far out onto the glacier. They are very dangerous, however, often fatal. The sun can also be a catalyst to break off a serac, cornice or other piece of ice. This can start a general avalanche down a steep face. The destructive power of these avalanches can extend several hundred yards out onto level glaciers. For this reason climbing near large faces at lower elevations is best done after 6:00 pm. It will be necessary to climb beneath potential avalanche slopes on many routes.

Hanging glaciers are the source of most of the largest avalanches to be seen. Avalanches from hanging glaciers at the top of an 8,000' (2400 m) or higher face can extend a mile or two (1.6 km to 3.2 km) from the face. The writer has seen the snow cloud of such an avalanche come out five miles (8 km). To see such an avalanche is unforgettable. The danger in these big avalanches, assuming one is not actually climbing the avalanche face, is not the blown snow which is so spectacular but ice blocks carried by the avalanche cloud. Fortunately the heavy ice blocks travel much less than the visible avalanche cloud. In general, the threat of large hanging glaciers is obvious. Moreover, the avalanche danger zone can usually be seen from ice blocks strewn on the glacier. Avalanche debris, however, is not a guarantee of the distance that avalanches can extend. All slopes within a mile (1.6 km) of a big face are potentially vulnerable. The greatest care must be used in placing campsites. A large crevasse in front of the campsite, while it may encourage the party to sleep well, will not be much protection in a big avalanche. Hanging glaciers can break off at any time. There seems to be a slight tendency for more activity at dawn and dusk when the ice begins to melt or refreeze. Heavy snowstorms also activate hanging glaciers.

An important difference exists between avalanches that start high above the climber and those which are climber induced. The climber must be continually concerned with the condition of the slope being ascended. Very rarely does a slope not give an indication that it is right for an avalanche. Completely unconsolidated powder and a hard windslab over an unconsolidated base are obvious. More difficult to evaluate is a heavy but deep snow, uniform in consistency, that is partially consolidated. As a general rule, but not always unfortunately, most slopes in Alaska are safe 24 hours after a snow storm. The wind does a pretty good job of consolidation. Only when the snow falls and settles without a wind is there likely to be a danger for several days.

Most steep slopes slide during snow storms. This causes few problems as the condition is obvious. The practical problem is how soon after the snow stops falling can climbing begin. In practice the steepest slopes will be safe simply because falling snow can not accumulate to any depth without sliding. Slopes exceeding 55° cannot accumulate large quantities of powder snow. Thus these will be clean as soon as the snow stops. Wind conditions during the storm will determine whether a 45° slope will be immediately safe. The most dangerous slopes are those 30° to 35°. At this angle snow can accumulate. Yet the angle is steep enough so that there is still a strong downward force on the slope. If a climber breaks the adhesion of the slope by step kicking, the whole slope can go. Although it is not common, the right conditions of wind and temperature can make such a slope dangerous for several days. Once slopes under 25° begin to consolidate at all there is little danger of their sliding. To repeat — the really dangerous slopes are those steep enough to slide but not steep enough to slide spontaneously in a storm without wind.

Crevasses and cornices pose the same problems in Alaska as elsewhere. The crevasses are bigger perhaps but crevasse patterns are fairly consistent and not too difficult to analyse. As in other areas the center or lowest portion of the glacier is often the least crevassed. A common mistake is to forget the size of a glacier and try to cut an inside corner too sharply. The error of this will be quickly obvious.

Cornices tend not to be as much of a problem in Alaska as in South America — some individual routes notwithstanding. Double cornices are rare partly because wind patterns are quite consistent.

The record of frostbite injuries is appallingly high. Poor leather boots are usually blamed but the improper use of equipment and poor judgment are probably more responsible. Failure to wear overboots, when the use of overboots would restrict climbing, failure to wear sufficient clothing on other parts of the body and failure to keep the feet moving during long belays — these can all lead to unnecessary frostbite. Tight crampon straps can be a factor, although loos crampon straps can cause other problems. Keeping the neck and ears warm can help greatly to reduce the danger of frostbite to the feet. It is the writer's opinion that the contributing factor in many cases of frostbite is either fatigue or lack of food. A shortage of sleep may also be a contributing factor. When the body is healthy and the climber is using reasonably good equipment intelligently, frostbite is difficult to get. For the treatment of frostbite, all Alaskan climbers should read Bradford Washburn's pamphlet, *Frostbite, What it Is, How to Prevent It, Emergency Treatment,* (Museum of Science, Boston, 1963).

One danger not often thought of in connection with climbing is river crossings. This does apply to parties walking in. It has particular importance for those walking into the north side of Mt. McKinley. Here the McKinley River and several smaller streams must be crossed. While it doesn't show up in the accident report, a very large percentage of those crossing the McKinley River have had close calls. If a climber falls while carrying a heavy pack, he or she can be rendered helpless. Use of a rope when crossing a fast moving river is almost mandatory. For the record, the history of parties that have tried to raft down some of the glacial Alaskan rivers has been almost universally bad. It is exciting but definitely dangerous.

Camp beneath Mt. St. Elias (Barbara Lilley photo)

EXPEDITION EQUIPMENT

Tents
Whisk Brooms
Sponges
Stoves
Fuel
Fuel Containers
Stove Primer
Cook Sets
Pot Grippers
Matches
Foam Pad
Large Spoons
Climbing Rope
Fixed Rope
Parachute Cord
Dead Men
Pickets

Spare Equipment
Ice Axe
Crampons
Sleeping Bag
Tent Poles
Tent

Pitons — Rock and Ice
Carabiners
Hammers
Shovels
Snow Saws
Wands
Large Tarps
Plastic Bags
Signal Mirror & Smoke Flares
Long Pole
Thermometer
Radio (?)
Walkie Talkies (?)
Medical Kit
Sleds

Tool Kit
Screwdriver
Pliers
Adjustable Wrench
Wire and Duct Tape
Needle and Thread
Hose Clamps
File
Glue
Straps
Stove Parts

Comments on Expedition Equipment

The three to four person dome style tent is the most comfortable and convenient tent for Alaskan use. The floor space of this tent is large, but most Alaskan routes have large campsites. Its high walls shed snow easily. Because of its height this tent is more vulnerable to wind than a regular two person mountain tent. One practical drawback to this tent is the erecting and fitting of a large number of poles. The poles tend to stick in cold weather. Also, in the event that one pole section is lost, the tent is rendered practically useless. A spare set of poles must be carried.

Most climbers find a low, two person mountain tent

depressing to live in over a long expedition. Such a tent can withstand much worse winds than a dome tent but it will require shoveling more often during heavy snowstorms.

Most campsites will be on snow. Ordinary tent stakes will be useless. Ice axes and rappel pickets will work well. Snowshoes, packs and buried food boxes can also be used. Pie plates, disks about six inches in diameter, are quite effective when buried in the snow but they can be difficult to remove.

Even if a tent is to be used at low elevations where rain might be expected, it should not be waterproofed as the tent will not breath. (See *Accidents in American Mountaineering, 1959,* American Alpine Club, New York, pp. 22-24.) The tent must be kept reasonably clear of snow at all times and at least one air vent should remain open.

Some climbers find dark colored tents depressing, particularly during long storm induced confinements.

A whisk broom and sponge should be left in each tent at all times.

The three types of stoves used are kerosene, gasoline and butane. All three fuels have faults. Kerosene is a powerful and efficient fuel. It seems to work well up to 20,000' (6100 m). The major problem with kerosene is that it has unpleasant fumes. This problem can usually be kept down to tolerable limits by careful cleaning of the fuel hole. Kerosene stoves also have many small parts which can be lost.

As a fuel, gasoline is about as efficient as kerosene and its fumes are much less noxious. While there is no scientific reason why gasoline stoves should have problems at high altitudes, they seem to be more tempermental above 15,000' (4600 m). A more serious problem is that a gasoline stove can flame up and explode. This, of course, shouldn't happen if the stove is used properly but most expeditions using gasoline probably have had at least one close call. Kerosene stoves are much less likely to explode when malfunctioning.

Another problem with gasoline stoves is that stove and lantern fuel has a tendency to clog at temperatures below -10°F (-23°C), due to frozen waxes in the fuel. This is a problem with stoves that have the fuel tank separate from the burner. With these stoves, it may be necessary to prewarm the fuel (under a jacket, in a sleeping bag, or by pouring warm water over the bottle) before use.

Butane stoves are almost always completely safe and they almost always work. In cold temperatures, however, the flame is not nearly as powerful as gasoline or kerosene. This adds substantially (50% to 100%) to an already slow cooking time. It also offsets the lower weight to burning time of butane. The power of a butane stove can be increased by pre-heating the fuel before use.

Stoves with a fuel capacity of one pint (½ liter) are recommended. One pint of gasoline or kerosene will last three to four hours, depending on the stove. As a rule of thumb, one-quarter pint (125 ml) of fuel per person per day is sufficient. Extra fuel should be brought to base camp.

One gallon (3.8 l) square sided fuel containers are the most convenient to carry, but must be removed from the mountains. Some climbers have had good experience with plastic bottles. Several one quart (1 l) containers should also be carried. (Make sure fuel containers and water bottles are properly labeled.) Obtaining completely leak-proof containers may be difficult, particularly for kerosene which produces gas when shaken. All fuel containers should be tested before use. Fuel containers should be carried upright when packed and it may be desirable to pack them in heavy plastic bags. The odor of kerosene on clothing is difficult to remove.

Small cans of lighter fluid can be useful for starting stoves. Heat tabs or fire ribbon also work.

Two cooking pots are needed for each tent or cooking group. A two quart (2 l) pot and a two-and-a-half quart (2½ l) pot are good sizes for cooking for up to six people.

A few closed-cell foam pads are nice for sitting on at base camp. A protective and stable base for the stoves can also be cut from this material.

In addition to personal utensils, there should also be a few large spoons, a couple of soup ladles and possibly an egg beater.

All climbing ropes should be the same length, preferably 150 feet (45 meters). Nine millimeter or 3/8" ropes are preferable on most routes to larger diameter ropes. It is not unusual for ropes to absorb water, freeze and become very heavy. "Waterproof" or "dry" ropes are prefered.

Five-sixteenth inch or 7 mm polypropylene rope is commonly used for fixed rope. This size works well with mechanical ascenders, and it is lighter than 3/8" or 9 mm. Weight may be a factor if large quantities of fixed rope are to be carried. A spool of 1,200' (365 m) of 5/16" (7 mm) polypropylene rope weighs 75 lbs. (34 kg).

In estimating how much fixed rope will be needed, a safe rule of thumb is 2 to 2½ feet of fixed rope for each *vertical* foot of the route that is to be fixed. (Or 2 to 2½ meters of fixed rope per vertical meter). If a route has not been climbed before it is likely that fixed rope will be desired somewhere that was not obvious in a study of photographs.

Although most of the best routes were first climbed with the use of fixed rope, there is some dispute over the ethics of using fixed rope. It can be stated as a fact that it would be inefficient and possibly unsafe to carry loads over some of the better new and existing routes without fixed ropes. On the other hand, a climber was killed on the Cassin Ridge of McKinley while using a fixed rope that was found in place. Its age was unknown, the climber trusted it, and he fell to his death. Whether fixed rope is overused on slopes where it is not needed is another issue. Even when overused, however, fixed rope usually speeds up a party. Whether to leave fixed rope in place or whether to pick it up and reuse it is still another controversial question. Weightwise and financially there is much to be said for reusing fixed rope. If the route is to be descended, however, the replacement of pitons and rappel ropes will be time consuming. Traverse slopes would require releading. Fixed ropes in place can be tremendously convenient in the event of an accident and evacuation. At one time there were twelve separate fixed ropes in the Japanese couloir of the Cassin Ridge on Mt. McKinley. Denali National Park now forbids any fixed rope to remain in the park.

Parachute cord is the all purpose fixer. Two hundred to three hundred feet (61 m to 91 m) is often used.

Rappel pickets can be cut from either 'L' or 'T' shaped aluminum stock. The length of the picket used will depend on the hardness of the snow. Sizes range from 1½ to 4 feet

Climbing a fixed rope on McArthur Peak
(Barbara Lilley photo)

(45 cm to 1.2 m) in length. A mixture of sizes is recommended. Holes for slings or hero loops should be drilled prior to the expedition.

If pitons are to be left in place, the use of chromemolly pitons will be expensive. Three or four hammers are sufficient for an expedition.

At least one snow shovel must be at every occupied campsite at all times. One large shovel is desirable for powder snow whereas a smaller and firmer shovel is needed to cut hard snow. A total of three shovels is recommended if there is any chance of the party splitting up. Warning: snow shovels break.

The ice saw is primarily an emergency tool to cut hard snow blocks for a snow cave or igloo should the tents be destroyed. Pure ice must be cut with an ice axe. Any bladed saw will do but a firm lightweight blade is best. The saw should have a protective cover.

Wands to mark the route are usually 4 foot (1.2 m) long ordinary bamboo garden stakes. To reduce melting out at low elevations some of the wands, which are normally painted green, can be painted white. This works only moderately well and makes the wands harder to see in a whiteout which is when they are needed. Deep placement of wands is recommended below 10,000' (3000 m) although there is a danger of the wands being buried by heavy snow. Wands should be placed no further than one rope-length apart. Changes in route direction or dangerous crevasses should be marked clearly as should the start and end of each fixed rope series. A rule of thumb estimate for the number of wands needed is fifty for each horizontal mile (1.6 km) plus one for each hundred vertical feet (30 vertical meters) of the route. Some sections of the route may not need marking but there is a tendency to underestimate and not overestimate the number of wands needed. Incidentally, a handful of wands works adequately as a tent stake.

Large tarps, at least twelve feet (3.6 m) square, are used to keep caches dry. Black plastic tarps are used to melt snow.

Several hundred plastic bags are needed to pack all non-canned foods within the food boxes. A large plastic

On the East Buttress of Mt. McKinley (Bill Krause photo)

bag may prove useful to store snow for cooking inside the tent. Large plastic bags are used for latrines.

An eight or nine foot (2.4 m or 2.75 m) bamboo pole can be used to mark the base camp cache. This will locate the cache even if heavy snow should fall. A collapsible metal pole may be desirable to mark the top of an important fixed rope.

Many expeditions have utilized plastic sleds to facilitate load-carrying during approaches over flat glaciers. This allows more weight to be carried between camps than by normal backpacking. There have been two fatalities in crevasse falls involving the use of sleds, and this must be weighed in comparison with their convenience. A method to keep the sled from being dragged into a crevasse by a falling climber must be utilized.

It is not impossible to lose or destroy any piece of equipment. Except for an item such as boots, which are probably irreplaceable, consideration of every contingency should be made so that no one's safety nor the success of the expedition is endangered by the loss of a single item. Some losses are inevitable. At least one extra sleeping pad, one ice axe and a pair of large crampons should be carried high on the mountain. An extra sleeping bag, tent and tent poles should go to base camp.

The use of radios has been controversial. In practice, most radios have proven unreliable when used on the mountain and this can be worse than having no radio. A radio that is guaranteed to work can be useful at base camp to call the pilot when the party is ready to fly out or if there is an accident. This saves unnecessary check flights but the radio must work. The only radios that are truly reliable are too heavy to use above base camp. (The writer has used one that weighed 150 pounds (68 kg), including generator, but it worked). Therefore, if there is any chance that the party will traverse the mountain and not return to a base camp, use of the radio becomes impractical (or very expensive) since it must be left.

FM radios can be rented in Alaska and can be utilized to communicate with stations in civilization. These radios are generally reliable, relatively static-free, and it is possible to patch into the Alaskan telephone system and call for weather reports or make long-distance telephone calls to the expedition's creditors.

Citizen Band (CB) radios allow different parties to communicate with each other in the mountains, but are not as reliable while communicating with base stations away from the mountains. It is possible to make phone-patches with these radios, but the transmission and reception is not always static-free.

On the ocean side of the St. Elias Mountains and in the Fairweather Range marine VHF-FM radios are useful. These radios are generally used to communicate with vessels offshore which may be able to relay messages back to civilization.

All of these radios operate on line-of-sight and thus can only be used when high on the mountain while communicating with base stations. It helps to warm the radio and the battery before operation in cold weather.

Walkie-talkies are a luxury that won't be needed except possibly on very difficult terrain for load hauling, pulley systems or winches.

Icefall on the Newton Glacier (Barbara Lilley photo)

PERSONAL EQUIPMENT

Boots
Overboots
Gaiters
Socks
Vapor Barrier Socks
Crampons
Long Underwear
Trousers
Wind Pants
Down Trousers
Shorts
Undershirts
Shirts
Sweaters
Down Vest
Parka
Down Jacket
Mittens
Gloves
Scarf
Face Mask or Balaclava
Goggles and Sunglasses
Wool Cap
Sun Hat
Helmet
Pack

Ice Axe
Sleeping Bag and Cover
Vapor Barrier Liner
Air Mattress or Foam Pad
Snowshoes or Skis
Carabiners
Prusik Slings
Mechanical Ascenders
Climbing Harness
Sun Cream
Lip Balm
Camera
Film
Diary
Pencil
Book
Bowl
Cup
Pocket Knife
Spoon
Fork

Comments on Personal Equipment

The Korean rubber boot or double plastic mountain-eering boots are recommended. Ordinary single layer leather mountain boots, even with overboots, are a risk above 16,000' (4900 m). Korean boots are warm when the feet are moving, but the feet and socks will be soaking wet from perspiration. Difficult technical climbing is impos-sible in the floppy Korean boot but it is sufficient for the average Alaskan route. Climbers using these boots will need extra dry socks and should not wear wet socks while in a sleeping bag.

Well fitted overboots and crampons do not interfere too much with snow or ice climbing. The overboots contribute measurably to foot warmth, especially if they are insulated. Gaiters are mandatory in order to keep snow out of boots if overboots are not worn.

Vapor barrier socks will keep feet wet, warm and uncomfortable just as the Korean boots do.

There is a controversy about 12 versus 10 point crampons. In general, 12 point crampons are preferred if front point work will be done on ice. The disadvantage of 12 points (or 10 point crampons with front points forward) is that front points get caught on trouser legs. Of course good climbers shouldn't trip over their crampons BUT —. The writer has always preferred 10 points with the front points straight down because pure ice in Alaska cannot be cramponed above 10,000' (3000 m). The ice is too hard. Many climbers will disagree with this last statement until they try Alaskan ice. (See Lionel Terray, "Mount Huntington," *The American Alpine Journal,* 1965 (Vol. 14, No. 2), pp. 289-298). The writer also prefers 10 points for mixed climbing, but this is a matter of personal preference.

If overboots are worn, it may be necessary to have crampon straps lengthened.

Knickers are not recommended for any peak above 10,000' (3000 m). Knee socks, unprotected by gaiters or wind pants, can be covered with snow and get wet. This makes the feet vulnerable to frostbite. Ankle length pile, polypropylene, or wool trousers are recommended.

Down trousers are not essential but are desirable for technically easy peaks above 15,000' (4600 m). Their bulk will interfere with technical climbing, however. Some of the bulkier commercially made down trousers, which are the warmest made, are more suited to the Antarctic than technical Alaskan climbs.

Down vests are nice but optional.

A front zipper is desirable on the parka.

Rarely used while climbing or load carrying, a down jacket is most needed around camp and for emergency bivouacs. While a luxury item most of the time, the comfort that it can provide adds measurably to the morale of the individual.

At least two pairs of mittens, possibly three, should be carried. The outer shells will often freeze into rock hardness and it may not be possible to thaw them. Therefore it may be desirable to carry an extra outer shell. Mittens are as easily lost as any item of equipment. A spare pair should be immediately available (not buried deep in the pack) at all times. Some climbers sew a pair of mittens to their parka. This may be inconvenient if the mittens become frozen and unusable. A more practical idea is to attach the gloves with a long cord and put the cord through the sleeves of the parka.

Down mittens are warm when dry but they will lose insulation when wet, and they will be wet most of the time. A shell over a heavy woolen inner mitten is more practical.

A pair of fingered gloves may be useful around camp but they can be dangerous if used for high altitude climbing.

Continuous exposure of fingers to cold dry air can result in "cracked" finger tips. This can be quite painful. Use of a light silk glove seems to help prevent this without interfering with finger dexterity. Silk seems to be warmer when wet than rayon or nylon. Most of the silk gloves available will fall apart with any heavy use.

Those climbers sensitive to the sun may want a wide brimmed hat. This is in addition to a wool cap which can be used for ear covering.

Some face protector should always be carried for possible emergency use above 10,000' (3000 m). Frostnip of the face, nose or ears is common and usually unnecessary.

Several commercially made aluminum pack frames are good. The type of carrying sack to use is much more controversial. It is recommended that the sack be permanently attached to the frame. The writer likes a big sack in which he can stuff every article being carried. Outside tie-ons cannot be recommended. Long strings are unpleasant to handle with fingers on cold windy days. Even well tied articles can work loose and fall off. Outside tie-ons are likely to come off during a fall. It can be disasterous if a tied on sleeping bag or tent comes off on a steep slope. Since loads tend to be bulky, the largest sack available is usually best, even though some compact heavy loads may not be balanced perfectly. Compartments within a sack get in the way with bulky expedition loads.

Controversial points about ice axes: Should they be long or short? Should there be a wrist strap? In some climbing regions the argument for a short ice axe is that it is useful on very steep ice and does not get in the way as much when doing mixed snow, ice and rock climbs. Most Alaskan routes, however, are not similar to typical routes in the Alps or the Canadian Rockies. Alaskan climbing includes a lot of glacier walking and moderately steep snow. For this type of climbing the longer axe is more convenient. The longer axe is also better for belays in soft snow. For side hill step cutting and descending on steep snow the long axe is definitely more comfortable. If the route has a large quantity of very steep (over 60°) climbing, one short axe can be carried by the route leader. Presumably once the lead is done, fixed rope will be placed and ice axes will no longer be needed. Ice axes, including long ones, can be carried conveniently in or on the outside of most packs with a small ice axe attachment.

It is the writer's opinion that there are only two legitimate reasons for using an ice axe without a wrist loop: conceit and lack of experience. The popular mythology says that good climbers won't ever lose their ice axes. In my opinion the perpetrators of this falsehood have done mountaineering safety a great disservice. Those who drop unexpectedly through a crevasse would be lucky not to drop their ice axes. The same is true on a cornice or in any fall. There is no assurance that the climber won't be momentarily winded or knocked unconscious. Of course, if one assumes that he or she will never fall, then the rope isn't needed either. The tendency for mittens to freeze solid makes it quite possible to drop an axe even without a fall. The danger of an uncontrolled ice axe causing physical damage to the climber exists but recorded injuries of this nature are rare — rarer than punctures from pitons. If some climber insists on climbing without a wrist strap, it is suggested that a second spare axe be carried at all times.

Air mattresses do have to be blown up at each camp and they can leak. Foam pads are foolproof and are very comfortable if a sufficiently thick (1½" or 4 cm) pad is used. Unfortunately, foam pads are very bulky, a serious problem for load carrying. A less thick pad is hard and cold for most people. Remember that even mildly uncomfortable sleeping conditions will have an adverse cumulative effect at high altitude. A three-quarter length air mattress or foam pad is not recommended. The feet are most susceptible to cold inside the sleeping bag than any other part of the body. They need a soft surface for resting. Susceptibility to cold and cold feet at high altitude are as much a function of the environment as the temperature. Those who sleep cold normally may want to use a thin (¼" or 5 mm) foam pad over an air mattress to reduce the effect of air currents moving within the mattress. Not all climbers will need this.

Many, if not most, Alaskan routes will have some low altitude walking on glaciers where snowshoes or skis will be useful. This can be determined from photographs. Any snowshoe will do but Yukon trail shoes are nice if available. Snowshoe crampons are worth their weight in gold. Skis can be faster and easier than showshoes but are obviously more dangerous on a glacier because of crevasses. Only expert skiers should use them. Unless every member can ski it is more practical if snowshoes are used by all.

Prusik slings are more easily attached to the rope before rather than after a fall. Mechanical ascenders are convenient but are not 100% reliable in icy conditions.

Many cameras, particularly those with focal plane shutters, freeze at low temperatures. Complete winterizing is effective but expensive. It is recommended that all cameras (and the radio) be stored in dry plastic bags while inside tents. Condensation inside the tent can easily cause camera trouble. Lens fogging will be a problem if pictures are taken inside the tent. Warm the camera first in a sleeping bag. Shoot the picture as fast as you can and replace the camera in the plastic bag.

A light meter is almost essential for dawn, dusk, and heavy shadow photography. A sky filter will eliminate the dark blue color characteristics of many mountain photographs.

The best climbers/photographers are usually those who carry lots of film and who shoot constantly. One roll of film per day can easily be shot.

Since Alaskan climbing almost always entails lots of bad weather, reading material becomes quite popular. Each book carried should be of general interest. It is questionable whether poetry in the German language or physics textbooks qualify as general interest reading. While the writer makes no moral judgment of the practice, books emphasizing sex and violence are always popular.

The Moose's Tooth (Bill Krause photo)

FOOD

Expeditions now generally recognize the important effect food can have on morale as well as physical condition. Although every effort is made to reduce total weight, this is accomplished by using dehydrated foods rather than by reducing daily food portions. Expedition work requires increased, not decreased calorie intake. Normally, the appetite of an Alaskan climber is ravenous, but the climber must force himself or herself to eat even if he or she doesn't feel like eating. Food monotony can lead to loss of appetite. Thus, variety in all food types and flavors is important. One or two food luxuries, such as a can of fruit, though heavy, can be great morale builders. To repeat: food should be filling and varied.

Almost all desired food products can be purchased at reasonable prices in Anchorage, Edmonton, Vancouver or Seattle. Only special freeze-dried foods, such as meats or eggs, need be ordered in advance. If driving up the Alcan Highway it may be best to buy food in Canada as there is a possibility that a Canadian duty will be imposed. Food can be purchased in Whitehorse but the selection may be somewhat limited and prices may be higher. Anchorage food prices are higher than food prices in Seattle but this can be cheap relative to wear on an overloaded car on the Alcan Highway. Some stores will give discounts on case loads or even the whole grocery bill. It usually pays to at least ask for a discount.

Food packing is a boring but important job. Three people can easily take twelve or twenty hours packing the food for a six to eight person expedition, so set aside the time. It's worth it on the mountain. The food should be broken down into expedition-day loads. All the meals for one day should be placed in a single bag. Every item needed, including paper towels, matches and salt, should be in one bag so that only one bag needs to be open at a time. Getting the right size bags is important. They must hold every item needed for each day and they must fit inside pack sacks. Measurement of the smallest pack bags is important.

All items in paper containers must be repacked in plastic bags. This includes powdered soup, cereal, packaged desserts, nuts, rice, etc. Several different bag sizes will be needed. Other items, notably cereal, sugar and salt may have to be divided into smaller packages. In this case two or even three plastic bags are needed to avoid breakage. Once packed, the bags should be permanently sealed until ready for use.

If there is going to be an air drop the food must be carefully packed. Sharp corners on carboard containers cannot be pressed against a breakable item. When filling cardboard boxes make sure that there are no empty spaces for food to rattle in or the containers may break. There cannot be any empty spaces. The boxes must themselves be packed with insulation inside another container, either a larger box or perhaps a flour sack. This outer container can break on impact but the inner box may be useful for carrying loads higher on the mountain, if it can fit in pack sacks. (A good box for six man-days of food is a 24-twelve ounce (354 ml) beverage can case, but these boxes are no longer generally available). A good pilot can make accurate drops from a low altitude but some pilots will drop from a higher elevation over a wide area. Allow for breakage and some losses. It is imperative that all of one item, such as matches, toilet paper or salt, not be placed in a single box. This also applies to non-food items such as hardware and fixed rope. If possible, fuel should not be dropped. If this is necessary, the only known container that has a chance is the five gallon (19 liter) jerry can, which must be removed from the mountains after the expedition. To be safe, drop twice the fuel expected to be needed, preferably in four large containers. Even if the jerry can breaks, there is a chance of saving some fuel if someone is on the ground during the drop.

A recommended food list and personal comments on the food follows. As food tastes vary widely, this can only be a guide.

Breakfast	**Quantity per man-day**
Hot Cereal	2 ozs. (57 gm)
Dry Cereal	
Powdered Eggs	
Dried Fruit	2 ozs. (57 gm)
Sugar	1½ ozs. (43 gm)
Powdered Milk	1 oz. (28 gm)
Soup	half package
Drinks	1 oz. (28 gm)
Cocoa	
Tea	
Fruit Drinks	
Salt	
Total Breakfast	9 ozs. (255 gm)

Lunch	
Chocolate	4 ozs. (113 gm)
Salami or Beef Jerky	2 ozs. (57 gm)
Cheese	2 ozs. (57 gm)
Dried Fruit	2 ozs. (57 gm)
Logan Bread	
Cookies	
Peanuts	
Hard Candy	
Mince Meat	
Jam and Peanut Butter	
Extra Cold Drinks (for water bottles)	
Total Lunch	12 ozs. (340 gm)

Dinner	**Quantity per man-day**
Meat	4-6 ozs. (113-170 gm)
Ham	
Canadian Bacon	
Roast Beef	
Salmon	
Tuna	
Meat Bars or Dehydrated Meats	
Chicken Dinners (dehydrated)	
Vegetable Stew	
Cheese (for glops)	1 oz. (28 gm)
Gravy Mixes	

Soup	Half Package
Rice or Potatoes	2 ozs. (57 gm)
Bread and Jam	
Gelatin Dessert or Pudding	Half Package
Cookies	
Applesauce	
Canned Margarine	
Canned Fruit (for base camp)	
Salt	
Seasonings	
Cold Drinks	1 oz. (28 gm)
Tea or Coffee	
Total Dinner	12-15 ozs. (340-425 gm)

Miscellaneous

Toilet paper, paper towels, scrubbing pads (without soap), matches.

Comments on the Food List

Depending on how much dehydrated meat is used, a good filling daily ration will be 2 to 2½ lbs. (0.9 to 1.1 kg) per person per day. Two and a quarter pounds (1 kg) is probably average. Some expeditions, by using only dehydrated foods at breakfast and dinner, have managed on much less than two pounds (0.9 kg) per person per day. Such groups have, however, tended to underfeed themselves and the food became boring because of the similarity of most dehydrated foods. Due to the definite benefit that good food adds to the morale and physical condition of an expedition, the writer prefers to carry more weight than most groups probably would. One factor to remember in setting food quantity is that a healthy climber will want and need much more food ten days after the start of a climb than the day when he or she arrives at base camp. Food satisfactory for ordinary weekend trips at home usually proves insufficient on an expedition.

Breakfast

Breakfast is the least exciting meal on an expedition, partly because all hot cereals are similar and basically tasteless. Oatmeal seems to wear best but it should not be eaten every day. Dried fruit in the cereal is liked by most (but not the writer) because it adds a flavor. Raisins, figs and prunes are the most favored fruits for long term use. Apricots, popular for many weekend climbs, lose their popularity with continuous use. Their tartness seems to aggravate sensitive stomachs. In general, dried fruit is one of the last eaten foods at higher elevations; some expeditions carry too much. A majority of climbers, but not all, prefer brown sugar over white sugar on cereals. It isn't fair to force brown sugar on those that don't like it, however. This should be checked in advance. In fact all food dislikes should be checked in advance. As a substitute for hot cereal, dry cereal can be eaten once a week for variety, and this always makes a big hit. Dry cereals aren't too heavy but their bulk is a problem for more general use. Powdered eggs make an excellent change for breakfast. Soup at breakfast as well as dinner is desirable. It is a hot liquid with good food value. Tea, coffee or cold drinks should be used in addition to soup since the climber needs three or more quarts (or liters) of liquid a day. Even though melting snow is a nuisance, patience is necessary because sufficient liquid intake is essential. Dehydration is a sure way to induce general weakness, frostbite, and possibly high altitude illness. A majority of climbers seem to prefer cold drinks to tea or coffee, especially coffee, but a few will have a strong desire for hot drinks.

Lunch

Lunch is usually a continuous meal, being munched bit by bit at each rest stop. Nowhere are tastes more varied than in lunch food. The one item almost universally desired is chocolate. The consumption of chocolate, particularly sweet chocolate, is likely to increase with altitude. Semi-sweet chocolate, often popular at base camp, is abrasive to stomachs at high altitude. Candy bars are a satisfactory variation although their food value is less than pure chocolate. Cheese, salami, nuts, sardines and various candies have their boosters and detractors. In general, spicy or highly flavored foods will be less popular at high altitude. One item always popular, although its food value may be questionable for its weight, is cookies. A home made Logan-type bread is excellent particularly with jam at camp.

Dinner

The two important food items at dinner are soup and meat. Hot soup is very welcome after a hard working day. To avoid monotony at least six different dried soup varieties should be used. Some foods can be used as a base for glops but the liquid must then be replaced by other drinks. Solid meat becomes very desirable on an expedition. Glops, though convenient to prepare, can become repellant and it may occasionally be desirable to fry meat separately. A significant weight saving (3-4 ozs. or 85-113 gm per person per day) can be achieved if dehydrated meats are used exclusively. The disadvantages of dehydrated meat are that they take a long time to prepare. The time factor is important. Individual dehydrated meats, such as pork chops or swiss steaks, seem to be more desirable in use than complete dinners. The other dinner ingredients are not easy to prepare in a crowded tent. Use of dehydrated meats will probably depend on the total weight of the expedition's food. Variety is important. Rice is generally more popular than powdered potatoes but neither should be used every day.

Miscellaneous

One roll of toilet paper *can* last a six person party two days. A large roll of paper towels *can* last three days. Paper can get wet. Paper should be packaged in plastic bags and taped shut. Extra paper ought to be carried. Some heavy duty scouring pads may be useful for pots with burned food.

It is not necessary or always possible to eat meals at times similar to those in "civilization." Some climbers prefer a big dinner before starting to backpack. Others want the big meal before going to bed even if this is early morning. If the summit day is likely to be at all extended, a full dinner before starting is not a bad idea.

Dinner on the Kahiltna Glacier (Bill Krause photo)

MEDICAL KIT AND FIRST AID

Because of the remoteness of most Alaskan mountains, evacuation is usually difficult. Assuming that the expedition has no doctor, first aid becomes aid for the injured before the doctor arrives, when the doctor isn't going to arrive. In fact, climbers must be prepared to give medical treatment, not just first aid. It is suggested that at least one member of every expedition familiarize himself or herself with common mountaineering medical problems and the proper medicine to administer in each case — in effect becoming the expedition doctor. A briefing session on all medicines being carried should be held just before going onto the mountain.

Medical supplies should be carried in at least two separate boxes. Where possible, split important drugs and supplies between two boxes. It may be desirable to have a third box with some basic items left at base camp. The two medical kits should be kept physically apart so that if one is lost the other will be saved. If campsites are split, have one box at each camp.

Drugs should be placed in plastic bottles. These bottles should each be clearly labeled with the *name* of the drug, its *general use,* the *dosage,* the *frequency of dosage,* and *restrictions* on its use. Drugs not used during the expedition should be destroyed within a year, unless a doctor says that a drug can be stored longer. Some of the drugs that expeditions will need require a doctor's prescription.

Drugs that require an injection are not recommended if the expedition does not have a doctor to administer them.

Some people suffer side effects from some medications. If any expedition member is known to suffer side effects, he or she must make this known to every member of the expedition as all can become "doctors" in an emergency. It is an excellent idea to list known allergies and side effects of the expedition members in all of the medical kits.

Vitamins are not believed to be necessary or particularly useful on an expedition lasting only a few weeks.

It is assumed that all expedition climbers are familiar with elementary first aid and are capable of splinting a broken leg or arm. An occasional review of a first aid book or even a practice session is an excellent idea.

Regardless of the seriousness of the situation, non-doctors should not practice surgery. This specifically includes appendicitis, the only treatment for which is rest and antibiotics.

High camp on Mt. Logan (Barbara Lilley photo)

Climbing to Russell Col on Mt. St. Elias (Barbara Lilley photo)

ACCLIMITIZATION AND GENERAL PHYSICAL CONDITIONING

It is not unusual for climbers, including those who thought they were in reasonably good condition, to feel weak and be at less than top efficiency in the first few days of an expedition. Mild headaches, coughs, restless sleeping and easy tiring are common. If the party has been flown to an elevation of 7,000 — 8,000' (2100 — 2400 m), acclimitization is often blamed. This may be a factor but there may also be another factor. This is "jet lag." Parties flying from New York to Anchorage gain six hours; those flying from Europe to Alaska gain eleven hours. The adverse affect on the body functions of this significant time change is well known among commercial pilots and diplomats. Probably similar to jet lag in its effect on the individual is the change from night to daytime sleeping. Most of the symptoms blamed on acclimitization can be induced by time changes and major changes in work, eating and sleeping habits. Rest is the best cure for jet lag or similar problems due to a change in living environment.

Acclimitization itself is a slow process whereby the body adapts to the reduced percentage of oxygen in the atmosphere. There is a small percentage of climbers who, for reasons unknown, have difficulty adjusting to altitude. The great majority adapt very well to the altitude found in Alaska *provided sufficient time is allowed for the acclimitization process.* After a day or two near base camp the climbers can begin to gain 2,000' (610 m) a day. Comfortable acclimitization to 20,000' (6100 m) requires ten days to two weeks for most climbers. One day maladies are not uncommon at any altitude during acclimitization and do not necessarily mean an inability to acclimitize. Climbers who are not able physically to acclimitize usually show signs of this by 12,000' (3600 m). Such people rarely feel well above this altitude.

There is no known way to speed acclimitization. Even being in good condition helps only slightly. Steady exposure to a gradually higher elevation seems to work best. An illness at high altitude can best be cured by descent to a lower altitude. Signs of pulmonary edema make descent to a lower altitude mandatory. Symptoms of

On the North Ridge of McArthur Peak (Barbara Lilley photo)

pulmonary edema include shortness of breath, cough with bloody or foamy sputum, general weakness, and a gurgling sound in the chest.

Both McKinley and Logan have been climbed by their easier routes in less than a week. Without exception, some members of these expeditions were very ill from altitude sickness. Outside of the fact that the expedition is physically unpleasant for those who become ill, there is considerable risk in pushing an expedition too fast. The chance of pulmonary edema is sharply increased. Speed records may have aesthetic appeal for some climbers but on mountains approaching 20,000' (6100 m), a rapid ascent defies nature. The aesthetics of speed records in this situation are lost on the writer.

Camp beneath Jeannette Col (Barbara Lilley photo)

ORGANIZATION ON THE MOUNTAIN

If the expedition sets a schedule of daily activity in its original planning, it would be well advised to stick to its schedule, if possible. In practice, unexpected obstacles will occasionally force a change in schedule but a realistic schedule should be possible to follow on most days. If there is no schedule, possibly because good photos weren't available in advance, then one should be made at base camp or at the start of each day at the minimum. The "let's see how far we can go" philosophy is bad practice. Climbers, like most people, are glad not to do today what they can put off until tomorrow. In practice, if there is no daily objective to push them on, they will accomplish less than what they are capable of doing. The daily objectives must be realistic. If the daily objectives are rarely obtained, then they will provide as little motivation as if there were no objective at all. Most climbers can be motivated to push on if they have a definite and realistic goal to reach. Although any single climbing day can extend ten, twelve or more hours, it is practical to set regular climbing objectives that should be accomplished in eight hours. Even an eight hour plan will regularly extend into a ten hour day in practice.

Every expedition needs a coordinator and someone to get it started in the morning. If the expedition has a leader, then this is his or her responsibility. The good leader is the one who can get the group moving without other members feeling that he or she is a dictator. That's no mean trick.

There are two general areas where expeditions get into difficulty on the mountain because of bad organization. One is lost equipment during snow storms and the other is not having the right equipment at each camp when the party is split between two camps. There is a lot more equipment lost than most climbers like to admit because they feel foolish about it. Most lost equipment is, of course, due to carelessness. It is difficult to lose equipment if every expedition or personal item is either in a tent or a centralized cache. When the weather is good there is a tendency to leave gear lying around the campsite. This is particularly true of crampons, ropes, stoves and pots. Should the weather change quickly or while the party is sleeping, articles lying on the snow can be quickly covered and lost. If there is a wind this can happen in minutes. A dangerous practice is to plant an ice axe and then place rope or crampons around it. A light snowfall covers the equipment on the ground, a person picks up the ice axe for a tent stake and the articles are lost. The only certain way to prevent such losses is to place everything in a cache which is covered by a tarp. Ice axes, ropes and gear can be used to hold the tarp down. Since storms will cover or fill tarps with snow it is desirable if one person makes a mental note of the placement within the tarp of equipment which may be needed, such as a full gas container. It is a nuisance to rummage through a whole tarp to find one item when the wind is blowing.

It is not impossible to lose whole caches. Low level campsites can be buried in five to six feet (1.5 to 1.8 meters) of consolidated snow while the party is higher on the mountain. Small caches placed between camps can be lost in a single day if poorly placed and marked. Needless to say, this can be serious if any cache has important items. It is not easy to protect caches at low level campsites from really heavy storms. The best that can be done is to pile the cache into as compact and as high a pile as possible. Wands should be placed around the cache and possibly, on top of it. To make a six foot (2 m) marker, place a single wand inside three wands and fix with adhesive tape. Two wands taped together are top heavy and can be blown over. Placement of caches is important. A completely level area is usually safe if marked. Steep snow patches are okay if near a prominent marker such as a rock (which itself must be easily seen in bad weather). One of the worst places is an open 15° to 20° snow slope. Drifting or sliding snow can accumulate to considerable depth here. Campsites are usually in protected and well marked spots, but temporary caches between campsites are often left in bad places (usually in haste).

The practical problem of organizing equipment for split camps is not easily solved. The job is to keep each campsite stocked with all essentials even if the campsite must be used when another campsite was desired. Ideally, all the equipment and personnel would move from camp to camp in a single carry. This can't be done. Not only should food be carried on the first load but as much expedition gear as well. The difficulty comes in leaving enough food at the lowest campsite plus required items such as stoves, tents and personal gear so that there isn't too much to carry up on the final load to each camp. Spare clothing not needed immediately should be carried during an early load. The same is true for fixed ropes and hardware.

If the party is split, one person must make sure that each occupied campsite has the following items:

> Tent
> One Stove (Does it work?)
> Fuel
> Stove Primer
> Two Pots
> Food (3 days absolute minimum)
> Snow Shovel
> Tarp

This is not a large number of items to keep track of but it is not difficult to overlook something. A common error is for several people to carry the same item high (particularly easy for stoves) only to discover that the item is no longer at the lower camp. This could be disastrous. Each expedition must devise its own system to prevent piling up of vital equipment in one place.

Piling up of equipment unintentionally can easily happen when the party plans to carry two loads between two camps but actually only completes the first carry. This can happen if someone becomes ill or tired of if the weather turns bad. It will also happen if the first carry takes longer than expected. Failure to complete the second carry occurs an average of once per expedition. Since the last carry tends to be a little heavier there is a temptation to carry important items, such as sleeping bags, on the first carry. This cannot be risked unless the ability to complete the second carry is 100% assured. For safety, the first carry of the day should be planned as the only carry. In this way, the expedition can't be caught short.

It sometimes happens that a lead party runs short of hardware, fixed rope or wands. Generally this happens because the amount of equipment needed was underestimated but sometimes not enough equipment had been carried to the high camp. The above equipment should have priority when carrying loads.

Fixed rope can be a nuisance. One thousand feet (300 m) is fairly heavy, but the average five hundred foot (150 m) face will require at least that. Uncoiling ropes on even a moderately steep slope is more than a nuisance. The big coils should be unrolled at camp. If the slope to be fixed has any uniformity, the rope can be cut into lengths equal to the climbing rope. Fixed rope can kink easily and it should be coiled carefully. The last length or two on a big coil may be badly snarled. If possible, carry the fixed rope over the shoulders. This will help prevent the rope from rekinking. If it must be placed in a rucksack, fold carefully and, most important, pull the rope out of the rucksack carefully to avoid a snarl. Some fixed ropes become such messes that they aren't worth salvaging.

The summit ridge of Mt. Logan (Barbara Lilley photo)

The "trail" from Denali Pass to the summit of Mt. McKinley
(Robert Somoano photo)

Camp on the Kahiltna Glacier, Mt. McKinley
(Bill Krause photo)

MOUNTAIN ETHICS

In 1966, the year that this report was first drafted, there were twenty-two climbers among five expeditions attempting Mount McKinley. In 1976 there were 508 climbers among 78 expeditions attempting Mount McKinley. In 1983 these numbers had risen to 709 climbers in 163 expeditions. These numbers refer just to Mount McKinley. The number of climbers and expeditions also grew exponentially throughout other mountains in the Alaska Range, Wrangell Mountains and the St. Elias Mountains. But the majority of climbers are on Mount McKinley and in 1983, 528 (or 74%) of those attempting McKinley were climbing the West Buttress. This traffic has resulted in a tremendous amount of litter, human waste, and unsafe drinking water from melted snow. This is not a recent phenomena. One climber noted that, "In 1969, the Kahiltna Glacier was such a mess that one could easily sight from the air where camps had been located."* In 1971 a party of seven burned 200 lbs. (90 kg) of paper, and removed 380 lbs. (171 kg) of garbage from the West Buttress route of Mount McKinley. A member of this party commented, "I want to attempt McKinley again, but not by the littered West Buttress route, which if it were not buried by tons of snow would look like a long centipede of garbage winding its way to the summit."** These problems are not as severe on other McKinley routes or other mountains in Alaska and the Yukon, but they exist and won't disappear until *every* Alaskan mountaineer makes the personal commitment to remove all of the trash and equipment that his or her expedition leaves on the mountain.

*Jeb Schenck, "Mt. McKinley — Littered and Overcrowded Route," *Summit,* Vol. 16, No. 10 (December 1970), p. 24.
**Terry Jones, "Clearing Garbage from Mount McKinley," *American Alpine Journal,* Vol. 18, No. 1 (1972), p. 60.

Litter

When planning food and fuel requirements prior to the expedition, repackage food and fuel into lightweight, collapsible containers. Cans and foil should be kept to a minimum and everything must be removed from the mountains.

Keep litter dry throughout the expedition. Keep it in a separate waterproof bag. Litter burning is usually very messy and should only be used as a last resort. With attention to weight and bulk during repackaging, and a strong commitment to leave nothing in the mountains, any expedition can carry out all of its litter without burning.

It is suggested that climbers notify the appropriate land-management agency (e.g., National Park Service or Bureau of Land Management) of the specific location, volume, and type of trash and debris encountered during their expedition. This information will help them direct volunteer groups and budget their own funds for clean-up projects.

Human Waste

Dig latrines as far away from established routes and campsites as possible. The pit should be eighteen to twenty-four inches (45 to 60 cm) deep. Insert a large plastic bag into the pit and collect feces in it. When the camp is broken, drop the bag into a deep crevasse.

To facilitate this operation, one McKinley expedition designed a seat that could be carried easily in a sled or pack. White its weight and bulk make it prohibitive for alpine-style climbs of steep routes, large expeditions (six or more climbers) on moderate climbs should give serious consideration to this easy and comfortable way of handling human waste.

Fixed Ropes

The placement of fixed ropes has declined in recent years due to the increase of alpine-style ascents of technical routes. All parties placing fixed ropes must remove them from the mountain after use. The removal of fixed ropes left by previous expeditions is another difficult problem. Often, an old fixed rope will have its anchor exposed, a portion of the fixed rope will be frozen in hard snow or ice, and a lower portion of the fixed rope will be exposed. If the upper portion the rope is cut and removed, leaving the rest of the rope 'anchored' in the frozen snow, ascending parties may trust the rope, with tragic consequences. Never use fixed ropes found on the mountain. Never leave any fixed ropes that your party has placed on the mountain.

Mountaineers now travel from around the world to climb in Alaska and the Yukon. Aside from transportation costs to Alaska, there is also a considerable investment of time and money to guarantee success on climbs. This report has attempted to show that with proper organization, an Alaskan expedition can be successful in attaining its objectives. Considering the commitment that Alaskan climbers make to ensure their success on climbs, there is no reason why climbers cannot make the commitment to leave the mountains clean. With proper organization, any expedition can remove everything it carries into the mountains and keep its impact to a minimum.

FINANCES

Raising money for an expedition is difficult enough. Fouling up the bookkeeping is likely to make the financial agonies worse. There is no excuse for bookkeeping to be a mess but quite a few expedition treasurers do an excellent job of fouling up their books.

It is recommended that one member of the group be appointed treasurer early in the organization. If possible, he or she should collect all funds from other climbers and pay all bills. One of the first jobs for the treasurer is to purchase a spiral binder. Two sets of accounts need to be kept: a record of actual expenses and a record of cash transactions between climbers. An advance to the treasurer (for example, $250 per person) is not an expense but is a cash transaction. One of the common book-keeping errors is for a climber to include cash transactions in expenses and thereby double account them. Expenses are only money paid to non-expedition members. The first page should record all actual expenses including a credit for any equipment lost on the mountain. Where possible, keep sales receipts in one place. The total of these expenses divided by the number of climbers is the cost per person. The cash transaction between climbers is only significant in the final reconciliation of accounts. Here is a sample expense statement for a four person expedition:

Expenses	A	B	C	D	Total
Glacier Flying	$950				$950
Food	720				720
Fuel	10	10			20
Wands	20				20
Shovels		40			40
Ropes			250		250
Total	$1,700	$50	$250	-0-	$2,000

Expenses per person: $2,000 ÷ 4 = $500

Cash transactions

Advance, April 1	($750)	$250	$250	$250
Advance, June 1	(750)	250	250	250
Personal Loan		100		(100)
Total	($1,500)	$600	$500	$400

Reconciliation of Accounts

Expenses Paid	$1,700	$50	$250	-0-
Cash				
Transactions	(1,500)	600	500	400
Net Paid	$200	$650	$750	$400
Expenses				
Per Person	($500)	($500)	($500)	($500)
Net	($300)	$150	$250	($100)

Both A and D owe money to B & C. Alternatively, A as treasurer can collect $100 from D and pay $150 to B and $250 to C.

This bookkeeping system is simple. If it is adhered to there should be no record keeping problem.

This list of expenses is not necessarily realistic for an average expedition, although it could be. Actual expenses will depend on how much flying is required, the amount and quality of food, expedition equipment, and transportation costs to Alaska. Another expense, though it won't show on expedition books, is the quantity of personal gear that each climber may have to buy. A large expedition can split group expenses into smaller individual shares and may be moderately cheaper per person. When estimating expedition costs it is wise to add about 10% of the total estimate for contingencies.

Mountain Ranges

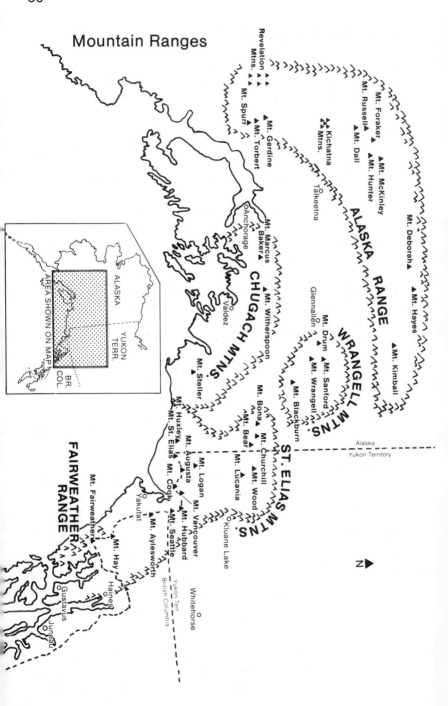

MOUNTAINS, ROUTES AND GRADING SYSTEM

Alaskan climbs cannot be graded by the same grading systems used in the continental United States. The difficulty of an individual pitch is relatively unimportant when evaluating a climb requiring several days to a couple of weeks. Whether the difficulty is encountered at 8,000' or 18,000' (2400 m or 5500 m) also makes a big difference. The length of the climb, the quantity of technical difficulties, the degree of objective hazards — all of these have a bearing on the rating of a climb.

There is no recognized rating system for Alaskan climbs at present. The writer has arbitrarily broken all Alaskan climbs into six different categories: Alaska Grade 1 through Alaska Grade 6 with Grade 6 being the most difficult. Most of the first ascent routes were Grade 1 or 2, a few being Grade 3. This reflects the fact that most Alaskan mountains have one fairly easy route technically and the easiest routes have been chosen for the first ascents. The first Grade 4 was the West Rib of McKinley in 1959. In 1961, the Cassin Ridge of McKinley became the first Grade 5. The Hummingbird Ridge of Logan in 1965 became the first Grade 6. In the future, there is likely to be a Grade 7 but at the present time Grade 6 is the maximum that can be climbed with reasonable safety. Grade 7 will probably have a very high avalance risk factor along with exceptional technical difficulties.

Verbally defining the six different grades is very difficult. It is more practical to list a number of climbs in each category. In general, however, high altitude climbs of technical difficulty equal to those of lower peaks are rated one grade higher. By definition, no peak over 17,000' (5100 m), no matter how technically easy, is rated less than Grade 2. This is because these mountains have expedition problems related entirely to height and cold. On the other hand, a mountain that can be climbed in one day has no expedition problems and is rated no higher than Grade 2, regardless of technical difficulties. In theory, a peak with some aid climbing could be rated Grade 1 or Grade 2 while a climb with easy fourth class rock climbing might be a Grade 3. All of the grades above Grade 3 involve good climbing. Grade 4 must have fifth class climbing on a high peak and upper level fifth and aid rock climbing on a lower peak. This is why peaks such as Huntington, the Moose's Tooth and Russell are only Grade 3. At their worst they involve only easy fifth class rock. Grade 5 must involve a fair amount of top grade climbing on a big climb and almost continuous technical climbing on a smaller peak. The west face of Huntington qualifies as a Grade 5. Grade 6 climbs have all the technical qualifications of a Grade 5 except that there are thousands of feet of these climbing problems. The only routes known to the writer that qualify as Grade 6 are some of the huge ridges of Mt. Logan.

A few typical examples of each grade are given below:

Grade 1: Dickey (West Face), Marcus Baker (West Face), King George (Southwest Ridge), Sanford (Northwest Glacier), Steele (Southwest Face).

Grade 2: Pinnacle Peak (West Ridge), Hayes (North Ridge), McKinley (West Buttress, Muldrow Glacier), Logan (King Col), Lucania (North Ridge), Foraker (Southeast Ridge).

Grade 3: The Moose's Tooth (West Ridge), Huntington (Northwest Ridge), Russell (West Ridge), Hunter (West Ridge), King George (East Ridge), McKinley (Pioneer Ridge), Logan (East Ridge), St. Elias (South Ridge).

Grade 4: McKinley (West Rib), St. Elias (Northwest Ridge), Sanford (South Ridge), Logan (Northwest Ridge), King Peak (Complete West Ridge), Hubbard (Southwest Ridge).

Grade 5: McKinley (Cassin Ridge), Huntington (West Face), Kennedy (North Ridge), Vancouver (South Ridges), Lucania (East Face), Foraker (Talkeetna Ridge), Dickey (East Face).

Grade 6: Logan (Hummingbird Ridge).

There is a partial list of Alaskan peaks and routes on the following pages. Accounts of the ascents can generally be found in the *American Alpine Journal* and the *Canadian Alpine Journal* in the year following the ascent. The grading of climbs is based on the writer's best estimate based often on insufficient information. These ratings are subject to change. An asterisk (*) indicates that the mountain or route is believed to be unclimbed.

ALASKA RANGE	Alaska Grade	Year of First Ascent
Mt. Spurr — 11,070';3374 m		
Southwest Ridge	1	1960
Mt. Torbert — 11,413';3479 m		
North Face	1	1964
Mt. Gerdine — 11,258';3431 m		
Hayes Glacier	1	1963
Revelation Mountains —	1-5	1967 & 1982
9,000'±;2750 m±		

This region is comparable to the Kitchatna Mountains, but with greater vertical relief. This area is a worthwhile destination for those interested in exploratory technical climbing in a remote area.

Kichatna Mountains —	1-5	1965, 1966,
8,000'±;2440 m±		1969, 1972,
		1975-1983

An excellent survey of climbs in this area is Andrew Embick's "Kichatna Spires," *American Alpine Journal,* Vol. 24, Issue 56 (1982), pp. 15-20.

Mt. Dall — 8,756';2669 m		
East Face	1	1970
Mt. Russell — 11,670';3556 m		
West Ridge	3	1962
Northeast Ridge	4	1972
Mt. Foraker — 17,400';5303 m		
West Ridge	2	1934
North Ridge	2	1983
Archangel Ridge	2	1975
Sultana Ridge	2	1979
Northeast Ridge	2	1966
Southeast Ridge	2	1963
South-Southeast Ridge	4	1976
Infinite Spur	5	1977
Talkeetna Ridge	5	1968
Southwest Ridge	2	1977

An unclimbed peak (Barbara Lilley photo)

Another unclimbed peak (Barbara Lilley photo)

ALASKA RANGE (continued)	Alaska Grade	Year of First Ascent
Mt. McKinley — 20,320';6193 m		
Muldrow Glacier	2	1913
Pioneer Ridge	3	1961
Wickersham Wall — Direct	4	1963
Wickersham Wall — West Rib	2	1963
Northwest Buttress	4	1954
Thunder Ridge	3	1982
West Buttress	2	1951
McClod's Rib	3	1977
Messner Couloir	3	1976
Southwest Flank	3	1977
West Rib	4	1959
Southwest Face — Canadian Route	4	1977
Southwest Face — McCartney/Roberts Route	5	1980
Southwest Face — Colorado Route	5	1983
Cassin Ridge	5	1961
South Face — American Direct	5	1967
South Face — Haston/Scott Route	5	1976
South Face — Milan Krissak (Czech) Route	5	1980
South Buttress — Thayer Route	3	1954
South Buttress — Japanese Route	4	1965
Lower Southeast Face (Isis) Face	5	1982
Upper Southeast Face*	5	
Southeast Spur	4	1962
Southeast Spur — South (Reality) Ridge	4	1975
East Buttress	3	1963
East Buttress — Catacomb Ridge	3	1969
Traleika Spur	3	1972

The North Face of Mt. Huntington (Bill Krause photo)

ALASKA RANGE (continued)	Grade	Alaska Year of First Ascent

Mt. Hunter — 14,573';4442 m

West Ridge	3	1954
Northwest Spur of West Ridge	4	1982
Northwest Spur	4	1977
North Buttress	5	1980
Direct North Buttress	5	1981
North Ridge	4	1971
Northeast Face & East Ridge	4	1966
Southeast Ridge	4-5	1973
Southeast Spur	5	1978
South Face and South Ridge	4-5	1973
Southwest Ridge	4	1978

This is possibly the most difficult mountain over 14,000' (4267 m) to climb in North America. If it were higher, the west ridge would be a Grade 4.

Avalanche Spire — 10,105';3080 m

West Ridge	2-3	1964

This peak is about ten miles (16 km) south of Mt. Hunter.

Mt. Huntington — 12,240';3730 m

Northwest Ridge	3	1964
North Face	5	1978
Northeast Ridge	4	1972
East Face	5	1980
East Buttress	5	1983
Southeast Spur	5	1978
South Ridge	5	1979
West Buttress	5	1981
West Face	5	1965

ALASKA RANGE (continued)	Alaska Grade	Year of First Ascent
The Rooster Comb — 10,170';3100 m		
West Ridge*	4	
Northwest Face	4-5	1980
North Buttress	5	1981
Northeast Face of Northeast Summit	5	1971
South Face and East Ridge	4	1979
Southwest Face of South Peak	4	1978
Mt. Dickey — 9,545';2909 m		
West Face	1	1955
East Face	5	1977
Southeast Face	5	1974
Mt. Dan Beard — 10,260';3127 m		
Northwest Face	1	1962
Southeast Ridge	4	1979
South Face	4	1974
Southwest Ridge	3	1978
The Moose's Tooth — 10,335';3150 m		
West Ridge	3	1964
East Face	5	1981
South Col*	4	
South Summit via South Col	3	1973
South Face	5	1975
Southwest Face	5	1974
Mt. Deborah — 12,339';3761 m		
West Face and South Ridge	3	1954
West Face Direct (three routes)	3	1981 & 1982
Northwest Ridge	4	1976
North Face	5	1977
Jensen (East) Ridge	5	1983
West Buttress of South Peak	3	1975
Hess Mtn. — 11,940';3639 m		
Northwest Face	1	1951
West and South Ridges	1-2	1967

ALASKA RANGE (continued)	Alaska Grade	Year of First Ascent
Mt. Geist — 10,720';3268 m		
Northeast Face	1	1974
Mt. Balchen — 11,140';3395 m		
East Ridge	1	1974
Mt. Hayes — 13,882';4216 m		
North Ridge	2	1941
East Ridge	2	1971
Southwest Face of South Summit	2-3	1976
West Face and North Ridge	3	1976
Mt. Shand — 12,660';3859 m		
East Ridge	1	1964
North Ridge	1	1977
Mt. Moffit — 13,020';3968 m		
Northwest Ridge	1-2	1941
Southwest Ridge	1	1977
McGinnis Peak — 11,400';3475 m		
West Ridge	1	1964
Northeast Ridge	2	1975
Southeast Ridge	2	1980
Mt. Kimball — 10,350';3155 m		
West Ridge	2-3	1969
North Ridge	3	1974

CHUGACH MOUNTAINS	Alaska Grade	Year of First Ascent
Mt. Gannett — 10,050';3063 m		
Northwest Ridge	1	1967
Mt. Goode — 10,610';3234 m		
East Face	1	1966
Mt. Marcus Baker — 13,176';4016 m		
West Face	1	1938
Mt. Witherspoon — 12,012';3661 m		
West Ridge	1	1967
Mt. Valhalla — 12,250';3734 m		
South Ridge	1	1957
East Face*	2-3	
Mt. Tom White — 11,300';3444 m		
West Face	1	1973
Mt. Hawkins — 10,700';3261 m*	1	
Mt. Steller — 10,617';3236 m*	1	
Mt. Miller — 11,100';3383 m*	2	

At the eastern end of the Chugach Mountains there is a group of mountains with fair vertical rises, which may be unclimbed. Mt. Miller, with a 7,000' (2133 m) vertical rise, should be the most interesting climb.

WRANGELL MOUNTAINS	Alaska Grade	Year of First Ascent
Mt. Sanford — 16,237';4949 m		
Northwest Glacier	1	1938
Southeast Ridge & South Ridge*	5	
South Ridge*	4	
South Face*	4-5	
Southwest Rib	3	1980

This easily accessible mountain has several fine route possibilities. The south ridge has considerable difficulties between 13,000' and 16,000' (3962 m and 4877 m). The southeast ridge and south ridge, if climbed together, would border on Alaska Grade 6.

Mt. Drum — 12,010';3660 m		
West Face	1	1954
North Face	1	1974
East Ridge*	3	
South Face*	2	
Southwest Ridge	2	1968

The east ridge has a series of interesting rock gendarmes and cornices. This is a good route for a party wanting a technical, relatively short and inexpensive climb.

Mt. Wrangell — 14,163';4317 m	1	1908
Mt. Jarvis — 13,421';4090 m	1	1967

West Blackburn Peaks (3) —		
11,000'±;3353m±*	1-2	

WRANGELL MOUNTAINS (cont.)	Alaska Grade	Year of First Ascent
Mt. Blackburn — 16,390';4996 m		
Kennicott Glacier	2	1912
Southeast Ridge	3	1974
South Ridge	4	1978
West Face*	4	
West Ridge*	3-4	
Northwest Ridge	2	1972
Northeast Ridge	2	1958
East Ridge	3	1982
East Blackburn Peaks (4) —		
13,000'±;3962 m±	1-2	1965
South Blackburn Peaks (3) —		
10,000'±;3048 m±*	1-2	
Castle Peak — 10,190';3106 m		
West Ridge	2	1978

Mt. Blackburn is one of the most impressive mountains in Alaska. Its west and south faces offer numerous route possibilities. None of these routes are technically easy and a few may border on Alaska Grade 5. On the south, Castle Peak and several other small but beautiful peaks offer climbing of moderate difficulty.

Regal Mountain — 13,845';4110 m		
North Ridge	1	1964
Northeast Ridge	1	1976
South Face and West Ridge	1	1978

ST. ELIAS MOUNTAINS	Alaska Grade	Year of First Ascent
Mt. Bona — 16,550';5044 m		
West Ridge	1	1930
South Ridge	1	1955
Northeast Ridge	1	1951
Twaharpies Peaks —		
14,000'±;4267 m±	1-2	1967 & 1977
University Peak — 15,030';4581 m		
North Ridge	2	1955
Mt. Churchill — 15,638';4766 m		
South Ridge	1	1951
Mt. Tressider — 13,315';4058 m		
Northeast Face	1	1969
West Ridge	2	1969
South Bona Peaks (4) —		
13,000'±;3962 m±*	1-2	

From a distance, Bona is an impressive mountain. In spite of its height, however, it is not an exciting mountain from a climbing standpoint. Some of its southern subsidaries (which may be unclimbed) are more interesting and one or two may reach 14,000' (4267 m).

Mt. Bear — 14,831';4520 m		
North Ridge	1	1951

Another big, easy, and not too interesting mountain.

Mt. Tittman — 10,000'+;3048 m+*	1-2	
Mt. Anderson — 10,770';3283 m*	1-2	
Mt. George — 10,335';3150 m*	1-2	
Peaks south of Mt. Bear —		
11,000'±;3353 m±	1-2	

To the south of Mt. Bear, between the Barnard and Chitina Glaciers, are a large number of small peaks, mostly unclimbed, between 10,000' and 11,000' (3048 m and 3353 m). These peaks have moderate climbing appeal.

Mt. Natazhat — 13,435';4095 m	1	1913
Mt. Craig — 13,250';4038 m		
Northeast Ridge	1	1969

ST. ELIAS MOUNTAINS (cont.)	Alaska Grade	Year of First Ascent
Snowfield Peak — 13,400'+;4084 m+		
East Ridge	1	1957
Mt. Strickland — 13,818';4212 m		
North Ridge	1	1957
Southwest Ridge	1	1973
Mt. Slaggard — 15,575';4747 m		
East Ridge	1	1959
Northwest Ridge	1	1973
Mt. Wood — 15,885';4842 m		
Northeast Face	1	1941
Southeast Ridge	1	1967
Southwest Face	2	1973
West Ridge	2	1959
Northwest Ridge	2	1969
Mt. Steele — 16,644';5073 m		
Southwest Face	1	1935
West Ridge	1	1969
North Ridge	2	1967
East Ridge	1	1967
South Face	2	1971
Mt. Lucania — 17,147';5226 m		
North Ridge	2	1937
East Face*	5	
Southeast (Harmony) Ridge	4	1977
Southwest Face*	3	
West Ridge	3	1969

There are several fine possible routes on the east face. The ridge which rises directly to the summit will be the most difficult and possibly the most dangerous. At the base of this ridge there is an icefall that is Himalayan in size. There are also some long unesthetic routes on the west side of the mountain.

ST. ELIAS MOUNTAINS (cont.)	Alaska Grade	Year of First Ascent
Centennial Range	2-4	1967 & 1972

To the south and southwest of Mt. Lucania between the Chitina and Walsh Glaciers, there are a dozen peaks from 10,000' to 12,000' (3000 m to 3700 m) in elevation. Several of these peaks rival the great small peaks of the McKinley region, such as Huntington, the Moose's Tooth and Russell. Very few of these peaks have easy ascent routes. Almost all of the ridges are sharp knife edges. There are a couple of months of exceptional climbing in this area.

Mt. Walsh — 14,780';4505 m

Northwest Ridge	1	1941

Mt. Queen Mary — 12,750';3886 m

Southwest Ridge	1	1962
West Ridge	1	1978

Mt. King George — 12,250';3734 m

Southwest Ridge	1	1965
West Ridge*	3	
Northeast Ridge*	3	
East Ridge*	3	

Unsuccessfully attempted at least three times, the east ridge remains a classic knife edge. The ridge rises in a straight line to the summit. The other possible routes may be as difficult but are not as aesthetic.

Hubbard — Logan Glacier Peak
— 11,750';3581 m*   2

To the east of McArthur there is an isolated and apparently unnamed peak. It is a little overshadowed by Logan but not so much that it deserves to be completely ignored.

Logan Southeast Buttress Peak
— 11,500';3505 m*   2

This prominent peak, on the ridge between Logan and Vancouver, is similar to but less difficult than Mt. Huntington.

McArthur Peak — 14,400'+;4389 m+

North Ridge	2	1961
West Ridge*	3	

The 14,000' (4267 m) east summit of McArthur has not been climbed.

ST. ELIAS MOUNTAINS (cont.)	Alaska Grade	Year of First Ascent
Mt. Logan — 19,520';5949 m		
Ogilvie Glacier	2	1925
Columbus Glacier — King Col	2	1952
Southwest Ridge*	3	
Western South Ridge	5-6	1979
South Face — Direct*	6	
Hummingbird Ridge	6	1965
Warbler Ridge	6	1977
East-Southeast Ridge	3-4	1967
East Ridge	3	1957
Catenary Ridge	4	1967
Independence Ridge	3	1964
Centennial Ridge	3	1976
North Spur	3	1974
Northwest Ridge	4	1979
Western Northwest Ridge*	3-4	
West Ridge	4	1978

The routes on the south face of Logan are the longest continuous climbs in North America.

King Peak — 16,971';5173 m		
West Ridge	2	1952
Complete West Ridge	4	1966
South Ridge	4	1969
Columbus Glacier Peaks*	1-2	

Immediately to the west of Mt. Logan there are several hundred square miles of small peaks (8,000' to 10,000' or 2400 m to 3000 m) surrounding the Columbus Glacier. To the north of the Columbus Glacier there are some interesting, though small, rock peaks.

Toland Peak —		
13,300'+;4054 m+*	1-2	
Mt. Huxley — 12,560';3828 m*	1-2	
The Hump — 12,375';3772 m	1	1981?

The last three hundred feet (90 m) of Mt. Huxley has the most pointed summit cone of any named peak in Alaska. There won't be much climbing but what there is should be fun. Huxley's neighbor, The Hump, is well named.

	Alaska Grade	Year of First Ascent
ST. ELIAS MOUNTAINS (cont.)		
Mt. St. Elias — 18,008';5488 m		
Newton Glacier	3	1897
Mt. Newton	3	1964
North Face*	3	
North-Nortwest Ridge	4	1978
Northwest Ridge	4	1965
West Ridge*	4	
Southwest Buttress	3	1978
South Ridge	3	1946
South Face*	6	
East Ridge*	4	
East Buttress	4-5	1972

One of the most attractive unclimbed routes in North America is the east ridge of Mt. St. Elias. It is long and has good climbing to over 17,000' (5200 m). The south face is at least 14,000' (4300 m) high with considerable objective dangers.

Mt. Newton — 13,810';4209 m		
North Ridge	2	1964
Mt. Jeannette — 11,750';3581 m		
East Ridge	1	1968
Mt. Bering — 12,075';3680 m*	1	
Mt. Malaspina —		
12,250'+;3734 m+*	1	
Mt. Baird — 12,000'+;3657 m*	1	
Mt. Augusta — 14,070';4288 m		
North Ridge	2	1952
Mt. Cook — 13,760';4194 m		
Northeast Ridge	1	1953

ST. ELIAS MOUNTAINS (cont.)	Alaska Grade	Year of First Ascent
Mt. Vancouver — 15,700';4785 m		
Northwest Ridge	2	1949
North Face	2	1975
Northeast Ridge	3-4	1975
East Buttress*	3	
East-Southeast Ridge	3	1979
Southeast (Good Neighbor) Ridge	3	1967
Eastern South Ridge*	5	
Western South Ridge	5	1968
West Face	3	1977

None of the routes on this mountain are easy and some of the new routes are objectively hazardous, notably the north face. The south ridges (at least two) of Vancouver easily rank with the south face of McKinley in length and difficulty.

Mt. Foresta — 11,300'+;3444 m+		
West Ridge of Southwest Peak	2	1979

Pinnacle Peak — 12,184';3714 m		
West Ridge	2	1965
North Ridge	2	?
East Ridge	3	1974

West Pinnacle Peak —		
12,000'+;3657 m+*	2	

Just west of Pinnacle Peak there is another peak that is very similar in countour.

Lowell Glacier Peak — 12,750';3886 m		
North-Northeast Ridge	1	1961

This peak is at the head of the Lowell Glacier opposite Mt. Alverstone and it is an easy walk for peak baggers.

	Alaska Grade	**Year of First Ascent**
ST. ELIAS MOUNTAINS (cont.)		

Mt. Kennedy — 13,905';4238 m

West Ridge	1	1965
North Ridge	5	1968
Northeast Ridge*	3	

Mt. Kennedy is the easiest mountain of its elevation in the Yukon. However, its north ridge offers one of the most consistently difficult climbs in the region. The ridge, mostly a wall, rises 6,000' (1800 m) at a steady angle exceeding 60°. This is a climb to challenge any climber in the world.

Mt. Alverstone — 14,565';4439 m

Cathedral Glacier	1	1951
Northeast Face	2	1967
West Ridge*	4	

Mt. Hubbard — 15,015';4576 m

Cathedral Glacier	1	1951
North Ridge	2	1974
Northern West Ridge	3	1976
Southern West Ridge	4	1973
Southwest Ridge	4	1973

Mt. Poland (or "Weisshorn") — 11,620';3542 m

Southeast Ridge	1-2	1976

Ulu Mountain — 10,250';3124 m

East Face	1	1972

Mt. Seattle — 10,185';3104 m

South Ridge	1-2	1966

Mt. Jette — 8,460';2578 m

Northwest Ridge	1	1975

Mt. Aylesworth — 8,700';2673 m*   1

Mt. Hay — 8,870';2703 m*   1

Mt. Lodge — 10,530';3209 m*   1

Mt. Watson — 12,516';3815 m

East Ridge	1	1974

Mt. Root — 12,860';3920 m

South Face	2	1977
Northwest Face*	2-3	

ST. ELIAS MOUNTAINS (cont.)	Alaska Grade	Year of First Ascent
Mt. Fairweather — 15,300';4663 m		
South (Carpe) Ridge	2	1932
South-Southwest (Transverse) Ridge	3	1975
Southwest Ridge	4	1973
West Ridge	2	1968
North Ridge of west peak, West Ridge	2	1977
North Face & East Ridge*	3-4	
East Ridge	3	1973
East-Southeast Ridge*	2-3	
Southeast Ridge*	2	(descended 1973)
Mt. Quincy Adams — 13,560';4133 m		
South Ridge	1-2	1962
Entire South Ridge	2	1973
Mt. Salisbury — 12,170';3709 m		
Northwest Face	3	1977
Northwest Ridge of South Peak	3	1977
Lituya Mountain — 11,924';3634 m		
West Ridge	1	1962
North Ridge	2-3	1975
Mt. Sabine — 10,405';3171 m		
North Ridge	1	1958
Northwest Ridge	1	1975
Mt. Wilbur — 10,821';3298 m		
South Ridge	2-3	1975
Mt. Orville — 10,495';3199 m*	2	
Mt. Abbe — 8,750';2667 m		
Southeast Face	4	1977
Mt. Bertha — 10,204';3110 m		
East Ridge	2-3	1940
Mt. Crillon — 12,750';3886 m		
East Ridge	1	1934
West Ridge	3	1972

ST. ELIAS MOUTNAINS (cont.)	Alaska Grade	Year of First Ascent
Mt. La Perouse — 10,728';3270 m		
West Ridge	1	1952
Northeast Ridge & Face	3	1959
East Face	3	1972

FURTHER READING

American Alpine Journal, issued annually by the American Alpine Club, 113 East 90th Street, New York, New York 10128 USA. Some back issues may be available.

Canadian Alpine Journal, issued annually by the Alpine Club of Canada, P.O. Box 1026, Banff, Alberta T0L 0C0 Canada. Some back issues may be available.

Cowals, Dennis, *Mount McKinley: A Climber's Guide,* The Mountaineers, Seattle, 1981. In English and Japanese.

Davidson, Art, *Minus 148°; The Winter Ascent of Mt. McKinley,* W.W. Norton, New York, 1969.

Hackett, Peter H., *Mountain Sickness: Prevention, Recognition and Treatment,* American Alpine Club, New York, 1980.

Houghton, John G., "Weather on Mount McKinley," *American Alpine Journal,* Vol. 17, No. 2, Issue 45 (1971), pp. 303-316.

Houston, Charles S., *Going Higher: The Story of Man and Altitude,* Charles S. Houston, Burlington, Vermont, 1983.

Moore, Terris, *Mt. McKinley; The Pioneer Climbs,* The Mountaineers, Seattle, 1981. A chronicle of ascents of Mt. McKinley to 1942.

Mountaineering: Denali National Park and Preserve, Alaska, National Park Service, U.S. Department of the Interior, 1983. Available in English, German and Japanese.

Mountaineering, Kluane National Park, Yukon/L'Alpinisme, Parc National Kluane, Yukon, Parks Canada, Ministry of the Environment, 1982. In French and English.

Perla, Ronald I., and Martinelli, M., Jr., *Avalanche Handbook,* Forest Service, U.S. Department of Agriculture, Agriculture Handbook 489, U.S. Government Printing Office, Washington, D.C., 1976.

Roberts, David, *Deborah: A Wilderness Narrative,* Vanguard Press, New York, 1970. An attempt on the East Ridge of Mt. Deborah.

Roberts, David, *The Mountain of My Fear,* Vanguard Press, New York, 1968. The first ascent of the West Face of Mt. Huntington.

Sherman, Paddy, *Expeditions to Nowhere,* The Mountaineers, Seattle, 1981. Contains chapters on the Centennial Range and Mt. McKinley.

Snyder, Howard H., *The Hall of the Mountain King,* Charles Scribner's Sons, New York, 1973.

Theberge, John B., ed., *Kluane Pinnacle of the Yukon,* Doubleday and Company, Garden City, New York, 1980.

Washburn, Bradford, "Mount McKinley (Alaska); History and Evaluation," *The Mountain World, 1956-57,* Harper Brothers, New York, pp. 55-81. Out of print but recommended. While this article is somewhat dated, it contains several ideas on climbing strategy that are applicable throughout Alaska and the Yukon.

Waterman, Jonathan, *Surviving Denali; A Study of Accidents on Mount McKinley, 1910-1982,* American Alpine Club, New York, 1983.

Wilcox, Joe, *White Winds,* Hwong Publishing Company, Los Alamitos, California, 1981.

INDEX